Y0-DJM-085

LOS ANGELES, CALIFORNIA

MUHAMMAD ALI

Christopher Riccella

MELROSE SQUARE PUBLISHING COMPANY
LOS ANGELES, CALIFORNIA

Consulting Editor for Melrose Square
Raymond Friday Locke

Originally published by Holloway House, Los Angeles.
© 1991 by Christopher Riccella.

All rights reserved under International and Pan-American
Copyright Conventions. No part of this book may be reproduced
in any form or by electronic or mechanical means including
information storage and retrieval systems without permission
in writing from the publisher, except by a reviewer who
may quote brief passages in a review. Published in the
United States by Melrose Square Publishing Company, an
imprint of Holloway House Publishing Company, 8060
Melrose Avenue, Los Angeles, California 90046. © 1991 by
Christopher Riccella.

Cover Painting: Jesse S. Santos

MUHAMMAD ALI

MELROSE SQUARE
BLACK AMERICAN
SERIES

CONTENTS

Chapter One

Desert Storm Begins

NOVEMBER 17, 1990: Muhammad Ali, the one-time Heavyweight Champion of the World, gets his bags ready to make a trip to the trouble-ridden Middle East, specifically to Baghdad, Iraq, on a personal diplomatic mission. Recent events there trouble him deeply.

Just three months before, the military government of Iraq, led by strongman Saddam Hussein, shocked the world community by invading the tiny oil-rich country of Kuwait saying that Kuwait was part of long disputed Iraqi territory and should be rightfully annexed. As word spread of the invasion, the United

Muhammad Ali laces up his gloves while mentally preparing himself for another bout in the ring. He was known for having great concentration over his athletic ability.

Nations began work on passing resolutions demanding the immediate withdrawal of all Iraqui military from Kuwait territory. Long a faithful and religious Muslim, Ali was extremely distressed by the trouble between the two nations that subscribed to his faith.

As the bloodshed began in Kuwait City, the capital of Kuwait, and main target of Iraq, visits by heads of state and diplomats to Iraq were quickly organized and launched, with the intent of attempting to get Hussein to withdraw his forces. The most prominent diplomatic figures to go to Iraq were Francois Mitterand, President of France, and Javier Perez de Cuellar, Secretary General of the United Nations. These attempts at stopping what would later be called "...the slaughter of the people of Kuwait..." would prove to be fruitless, but continued. At some point because Ali decided that perhaps the high regard in which he was held in the Muslim World could prove useful to the present advisors, he began sending out feelers to Saddam Hussein regarding a visit to Iraq.

Being a Muslim himself, like Hussein, Ali wanted to keep an open mind about the conflict. Ali knew, as did the entire world community, that whether Kuwait was annexed or conquered made little difference; innocent

Andrea McArdle, famed Broadway child star from Annie *helps Ali place his new Saturday morning cartoon,* I Am The Greatest: The Adventures Of Muhammed Ali *in the NBC Saturday Morning Lineup.*

people were dying.

Despite conflicting news coverage the news of the invasion that did come out to the world said the same thing: there had been a massacre. Men and women on the street, as well as Kuwaiti children in school, were indiscriminately shot and killed.

Before making his decision to journey to Baghdad, Ali did his homework. He learned that Kuwait, easily the smallest country in the Persian Gulf, had nearly eighty percent of the petroleum reserves there. Having no military, per se, Kuwait depended upon its membership in the United Nations to negotiate its position in the world community.

On the other hand Iraq had just completed the largest military build-up in its history. Having had the support of the United States and its Western allies in the Iran-Iraq War, the Iraqui army now ranked fourth in size in the world—certainly a force to be reckoned with.

Kuwait's political position was also at a precarious point. Just prior to the invasion, the government had been informally reprimanded by the United Nations for discontinuing free elections. The Emir of Kuwait closed Parliament and had begun to rule solely by his will, but no human rights violations had been made.

Nevertheless, the occupation of a defenseless Kuwait by Hussein's seasoned, well-trained and superior armed forces was a great offense to the world community and Ali knew it, but more importantly, felt he could do something about it.

Opting to avoid the questions of right and wrong in the direct confrontation between the governments of Iraq and Kuwait, Ali decided to make the object of his visit a peaceful effort to release American hostages held in Baghdad. He hoped that his world celebrity status and his religious beliefs as a Muslim-American would help him in his goal of releasing the hostages, as well as give him an opportunity to talk to Saddam Hussein about world peace.

In the meantime, the United States began a campaign in the United Nations to organize a world coalition protesting the invasion. Terik Aziz, the Ambassador to the United Nations from Iraq, defended the political position of his state—and his leader, the President of Iraq, Saddam Hussein.

By the end of September 1990, the coalition of nations was crystallized. It was not to be an exclusively Western effort, however. President George Bush of the United States, knew that Western influence (and political pressure)

A technique that Ali developed in boxing was to rear totally back so his opponent would miss his target giving Ali ample

time to then lunge forward for the blow. He's seen here using this strategy against George Frazier.

in the Middle East had been disastrous in the past and he lobbied for Middle Eastern support as well. The coalition consisted primarily of the United States, Great Britain, France, Germany, Japan, Italy, Saudi Arabia, Egypt, Turkey, and Syria—Israel conspicuously did not join the coalition. Statements issued by Moshe Arens the Israeli Minister of Defense, threatened the possibility of a separate war between Israel and Iraq, if Israel became a target of Saddam Hussein. This prophesy was fulfilled when Tel Aviv was attacked by SCUD missiles fired from Iraqui positions, but negotiations with the United States and the placement of Patriot ground defense systems to protect the city, restrained the Israelis from making their own strategic plans.

However, the original Israeli position alarmed the United States and the Coalition, because diplomatic solutions were still in the works, while military options were also being considered. The thought of an uncoordinated military action in response to the invasion of Kuwait made Bush and leaders of the World Coalition uneasy.

The World Coalition would have to move quickly.

Efforts made by James Baker, Secretary of State, and Dick Cheney, Secretary of Defense,

This is a closeup of Cassius Clay displaying the gold medal he earned in the 1960 Olympic games in Rome, Italy. He really didn't get along with the other fighters, but when the United States won the gold in boxing, everyone was happy.

had resulted in the military mobilization by the United States that would be known as Operation Desert Shield. This was implemented by General Colin Powell, Chairman of the Joint Chiefs of Staff of the United States, and would be led by General Norman Schwarzkopf. As military action began to be evident all Americans were ordered by Presidental Option, to leave Iraq.

In Baghdad, however, communications with the Embassy of the United States to Iraq, had been severed by Iraqui military. The staff quickly closed the United States Embassy, barricading themselves within the walls of the installation—a measure taken for fear of a recurrence of the United States Embassy takeover ten years before in Iran. Shortly after, temporary communication was restored and all personnel were permitted to leave Baghdad safely.

Early negotiations with Saudi Arabia, and its King Faad, proved useful, and their government immediately approved the use of all Saudi military bases by the United States and Coalition forces. American and Coalition troops, planes (including the F-117A Stealth Fighter and the B-2 Stealth Bomber), aircraft carriers, submarines, destroyers, and battleships were off to the seas of the Persian Gulf and the bases of Arabia.

Coalition and United Nations negotiations hit an impasse, as it became evident in a news conference statement made by Terik Aziz in early January. The escalation of Operation Desert Shield to Operation Desert Storm began.

Operation Desert Storm was the military force granted to the World Coalition by the United Nations. At that time, President Bush issued a January 15, 1991 deadline to President Hussein demanding that all Iraqui military personnel be withdrawn from Kuwait, unconditionally, and that the former government of Kuwait be restored.

The nations that pledged military forces by this time included: the United States, Great Britain, France, Italy, Egypt, and Saudi Arabia—where most of the half-million troops were now stationed. Japan pledged eleven billion dollars in military aid, while Germany pledged eight billion dollars along with military intelligence and hardware, while Syria and Turkey sent minimal troops and allowed Coalition air power to use their military installations.

Operation Desert Shield/Storm was the greatest military build up since the Vietnam War, involving more countries than the

Strolling down 7th Avenue in New York City, Cassius Clay attracts many of the different fans he had won over for his Olym-

pic victory. Clay was known to give out autographs and to take such walks with boxing fans.

alliances formed with the Allies and the Axis nations of World War II. This greatly concerned many Americans, including Muhammad Ali.

So the journey to Iraq by Ali was planned for November 17, 1990. He was accompanied by his ex-manager and public relations man, Arthur Morrison, and two members of the Coalition to Stop U.S. Intervention in the Middle East, an organization formed specifically to keep out Western influence in that part of the world.

Ramsey Clark, former Attorney General of the United States, and affiliated with the Coalition to Stop U.S. Intervention in the Middle East, said of the journey that the ". . .basic purpose was for peace and friendship. . ." as well as an effort to release the American hostages.

Aware of the January 15 deadline set by the United Nations when the recently formed World Coalition would be allowed to take any and ". . .all action including military force. . ." if Hussein had not withdrawn his troops, Ali left the United States on the 17th of November. At the end of a ten-day tour of Baghdad, on November 27 he spent fifty minutes of what was described as "friendly talk" with Saddam Hussein.

"There is a real fundamental relationship between Saddam Hussein and Muhammad Ali because they're both Muslim," says Lindsey Clemmell, a British filmmaker who was along on the trip.

Despite the fact that the champ had been plagued by a bout of ill health, he was able to get a successful message through to Hussein.

Commenting on this, one of the released hostages, Harry Brill Edwards of Fort Lee, New Jersey said, "He's quiet, but he's better than I expected. His speech is halting, but he's sharp. To make that long journey in his condition—he's just a tremendous human being."

Lonnie Ali, the champ's wife, issued a statement from Los Angeles saying, ". . . his symptoms are exaggerated. From what I understand, he is very, very tired." It was also known that he had run out of Thyrolar, the prescribed medication for his condition.

Ali was then allowed to leave Baghdad, taking with him some fifteen of an estimated three-hundred American hostages being held in Baghdad.

Commenting on the possibility of an armed conflict between Iraq and the World Coalition, Ali said, "This is the land of the Garden Of Eden, and the land where Abraham was born.

An early opponent of Clay's and later a cherished friend and trainer of Muhammad Ali was Archie Moore. Here Archie Moore strikes a publicity boxing-stance shot.

How could it be bombed?"

Ali's trip to the Middle East did not prevent
what would be known as the Persian Gulf War.
However his diplomatic efforts will leave a
mark that will forever be remembered on its
history.

Too, this was not the first time Ali had
undertaken a political mission. Amidst the
United States boycott of the 1980 Olympics led
by then President Jimmy Carter, Muhammad
Ali made a five-nation tour of Africa, where
he is a continental hero, to show solidarity
against the Soviet occupation of Afghanistan.

Muhammad Ali always works from an
unspoken set of principles and personal ethics
developed at the early stages of his life. He has
not always made the most popular decisions,
socially, religiously or otherwise. He has en-
countered criticism from both whites and
blacks alike. But it is his personal ethical code
that resulted in the development of a controversial man, one who is recognized as a
great American.

Chapter Two

Born A Fighter

O N A DRY, COLD JANUARY day, Cassius Marcellus Clay, Jr., came into this world a fighter. His parents were Odessa Lee Grady Clay and C.M. "Cash" Clay, Sr., and he was born in Louisville, Kentucky's General Hospital. The date was January 17, 1942, and the birth wasn't an easy one.

Because his mother's pelvis was too small and the baby's head too large for a normal delivery. Odessa was in labor for many long, painful hours before the doctors at last succeeded in using clamps to push and pull the newborn into the world.

A still from a 1977 television mini-series Freedom Road, *which chrolologized the life of an ex-slave and his rise to the United States Senate, during the Reconstruction Era.*

Odessa nearly died in labor, a fact that would cause guilt and tension between Cassius and Cash all their lives.

Because of the devices used in the delivery of the newborn, scars of birth were left on the baby's cheeks. It had been a difficult birth for both baby and mother, and the child was taken away by the nurse to be bathed, still screaming uncontrollably.

Shortly after, a quiet child was returned by the nurse. Odessa knew that this wasn't the screaming youngster she had let them take away from her. But in her tired state she held the baby, finally looking at its wristband and confirming that this was not her child—it had been almost fifteen minutes before she noticed the bracelets were wrong. They easily made the switch back and as the screams and wails became louder and louder from the hallway, Odessa breathed a sigh of relief—her son was being returned to her.

Cash Clay, fancying himself as handsome (he was) and romantic, wanted to name his first son Rudolph Valentino Clay, after the matinee-idol of silent film fame. Cash's own reputation was that of a man who was the proverbial romantic. He appreciated beauty in art, and in all aspects of life. But Odessa insisted that

Actor Chip McAllister, wearing number one, is shown here in a still from The Greatest *based on the life story of Muhammad Ali. Here young Cassius Clay recieves the gold medal at the 1960 Olympic Games in Rome, Italy*

their first son be named after her husband's father.

Cash wasn't to wait long for a Rudy Clay, though. Thirteen months later his second son arrived, and there was now Rudolph Valentino Clay in the family.

Both father and first son would carry the name of the famous nineteenth century white abolitionist and friend of President Abraham Lincoln; it has been said that Cash's father gave him the name in gratitude for the original Cassius Marcellus Clay's work toward ending slavery in the United States. But this was a bitter-sweet gift.

For years, Cassius, Jr., was told he should be proud of his namesake and honor the memory of such a great man. But later driven by the curiosity instilled in him by his father about this man, Cassius, Jr. sought out the writings of the abolitionist and showed them to his teacher, who had not bothered to read them before. The first Cassius Clay, although a staunch opponent of slavery, was a firm believer in white superiority—based on biological information such as cranial size and average weights of brains compared in cadavers of white and black men.

This discovery greatly disappointed the young Cassius and from then on, there would be no more talk of honoring the man whose name he bore—he was a white racist—however intellectual.

Cassius did love his father, however, and the fact that he shared his father's name made him proud. It was not until he joined the Black Muslims years later that he rejected any trace of the legacy of slavery. For a time, he was known as Cassius X, following the example of his friend Malcolm X.

Since most blacks in the United States after the Civil War would take the surname of the family they once served—or of the founding fathers, Washington, Jefferson and so on, the Black Muslims would use the neutral letter "X" in place of the false surname, or find a suitable African surname if one could be properly traced. It was later that the leader of his faith, Elijah Muhammad, would give him the name of Muhammad Ali.

The home where Cassius grew up, until he left at eighteen to become a professional boxer, was a modest bungalow at 3302 Grand Avenue, in the West End section of black Louisville. Of the three black sections in the city, the West End was and still is the most populated. The California Area is home to the black middle class, while the East End, also known as "Snake Town," holds the worst of the city's ghettos.

His father worked as a sign painter, traveling all over the city. A frustrated artist, he felt he had great talent. But because of the Jim Crow attitude that still existed in the South in the Forties and Fifties, the only steady work he could get was as a sign painter. Still, at a time when there was great unemployment within the black community, Cash always had respectable work.

His creative talents were not completely stifled, however. He was eventually commissioned to paint murals for many of the city's predominantly black churches. He bought the house on Grand Avenue in 1946 for $4,500, and later in life boasted that he had never in his life missed a day of work, ". . .and I never worked for nobody but me."

Later in *The Greatest,* Muhammad Ali remembers his childhood a little differently. He said that there was barely enough money to keep up the mortgage payments, none for necessary repairs. It was true that both the roof and walls leaked, and for eight years the porch was dilapidated to the point of collapse. Even temporary repairs would have cost two-hundred dollars, a great sum in those days, so the frame of the house was permitted to slump.

As his popularity in America began to skyrocket, young
Cassius Clay began to dabble in outside of the ring.
Here he is seen recording The Gang's All Here.

Although not poverty stricken, the Clay family never could afford a car that was less than ten years old. They couldn't even afford to buy new tires for the cars they did own. Much of the clothes the family wore were second hand, and Cash became adept at cutting cardboard to fit into the soles of their shoes to cover the holes—a talent he wasn't proud of.

Ali remembered that there was rarely enough money for both boys to have bus fare for school, and so he began to race the bus, on foot, to school. His mother didn't like this situation so she began saving up to buy him a bicycle as a Christmas present.

This special relationship between mother and son would last all their lives. Perhaps it was because of the close call during Cassius' birth. Nevertheless Cassius had a special relationship with his mother and "Bird," was the pet name he had for her, saying she looked like a bird—pert and pretty. The name was soon adopted for her by the rest of the family.

Bird Clay worked as a domestic for a white family in the Highland section of the city, cleaning and cooking and taking care of the children for four dollars a day. Usually she stopped at the local market on her way home and spent most of her pay on groceries for the day's dinner.

Heavyweight Boxing Champion Cassius Clay is mobbed by fans after making an appearance in the Roxbury section of Boston, to address a congregation of Black Muslims at the Temple of Islam.

Appearing at one of the many charitable functions he has sup-
ported throughout his career, Ali speaks to a crowd at a na-

tional event. By his side is "Sugar" Ray Robinson, a favorite boxing champion in his own right.

In turn, Bird's pet name for her first son is "GG," or just "G," because those were the first sounds she heard him try to speak. Later, Cassius swore that he was trying to say Golden Gloves. Whether this is true or not, it seems he was destined for the boxing ring.

Even as a small child, he was the leader of the other children. As Cassius grew a little older he ran with a neighborhood gang, which worried his parents very much. His street adventures never got him into serious trouble, although on at least one occasion, he came close to having trouble with the law.

Also, political events with the rise of the Civil Rights Movement, formulated many of his ideas of racial equality. One particular incident made him determined through boxing that he would not lie down and be treated like most other blacks of his day. That incident was the murder of Emmett Till.

Emmett was a thirteen year old black boy from Chicago accused of raping a white girl. Although all of the evidence against him was circumstantial, he was still accused—and there was great public outcry by whites for him to be tried. There was insubstantial evidence and the local law officials left it at that. But the local white supremacists had their own idea of justice.

Soon after he was abducted by white supremacists and beaten to death. He was heavily beaten about the head and shoulders, and then castrated. Ali told Jose Torres his feelings about the incident and how it changed his life in *The Greatest:*

"Emmett Till and I were about the same age. A week after he was murdered in Sunflower County, Mississippi, I stood on the corner with a gang of boys, looking at pictures of him in the black newspapers and magazines. In one, he was laughing and happy. In the other, his head was swollen and bashed in. His mother had done a bold thing. She refused to let him be buried until thousands marched past his open casket in Chicago and looked down at his mutilated body. I felt a deep kinship to him especially when I learned he was born the same year and day I was."

Cassius Clay became a rebel against the treatment given blacks by many whites under Jim Crow. After the murder of the boy, Emmett Till, he vowed to make a difference, to show those who had killed him that they wouldn't get away with it. One night he and his friend, Ronnie King, sneaked out and went down to the old railroad station on Louisville's

West Side.

The boys walked along the tracks throwing stones at a poster of Uncle Sam. The poster angered Clay, after all, Uncle Sam was supposed to preserve freedom for all Americans, wasn't he?

Then spying a vacant shoe-shine shed, they broke into it and stole two iron shoe rests. Under Clay's direction they planted the shoe rests deep between the rails of the track in hopes of derailing and destroying an unsuspecting engine coming down the tracks. They waited, and sure enough, a diesel engine soon came around the bend.

The engine hit the shoe rests and pushed them about thirty feet, ripping up the ties, before one of the wheels locked and the engine came literally to a screeching halt.

The boys turned and ran, but behind them they could hear the clamorous wreck when their act of sabotage was at least partially successful. Much damage had been done and it would be several days before the tracks would be usable again.

Cassius looked back, and saw the personage of the United States Government, Uncle Sam, in the poster. The picture seemed to be staring straight at him, and he would tell friends that he knew, that sooner or later, he would

A posed portrait from Ali's first marriage. The lucky bride is Sonji Roi. It was said that her refusal to stop wearing makeup and to start obeying the strict rules of Islam led to irreconsilable differences and their divorce in 1967.

have to confront the white goatee-bearded old man in the red, white and blue suit.

He went back to the scene of the sabotage two days later, and found the yard crew still cleaning up the debris. And a battered poster of Uncle Sam still staring straight at him, saying "I Want You!"

Cassius wasn't the only Clay to have brief clashes with the law. Cash Clay, according to Joe Torres, was a hard-drinking man, obviously a result from the frustration about his squelched talent as an artist. And he had his own share of problems with authority, which at this time was mostly white. He was arrested four times for reckless driving, twice for disorderly conduct, once for ignoring parking tickets, and once for disposing of mortgaged property. Twice he was arrested on charges of assault and battery.

The charges were never serious, and even Cash has said himself, ". . . heck, it's easy to get into a little scrape. But let them show where I've ever even spent one night in jail— they can't do it." This was thought an arrogant attitude for a black man and many thought that Cash was indeed, arrogant. This might have been a result of the fact that the Clays produced good-looking men.

The Clay's have a legacy says Cassius, en-

couraged by his father, and his grandfather
about how good-looking the men are in the
family. This vanity has made them a boisterous
group. This was the beginning of the loud-
mouthed reputation Clay would eventually get.

Cash was basically a gentleman, though,
following the example of his own father. He
never physically punished his sons, as so many
other children are. He wanted Cassius to be
either a teacher or a lawyer, but once he saw
him in the ring, Cash Clay was the first to
shout that his boy would be "The Greatest."

Chapter Three

To Be
The Best

W HO WOULD HAVE THOUGHT THAT the Christmas gift his mother had in mind for young Cassius would lead to his brilliant boxing career?

His boxing career began because his new fire engine red Schwinn bicycle was stolen. Cassius was riding his new Christmas present with his closest buddy, Johnny Willis, when it began to rain heavily; he was twelve years old at the time. Looking for cover, Johnny remembered a black business exhibition, part of the annual Louisville Home Show, being held at Columbia Auditorium. The auditorium is a recrea-

Muhammad Ali meets with reporters after a match. Always a vocal personality, these meetings with the press were sometimes surprising and could be very candid.

tion center at 4th and York, with a bowling alley and a gym for boxers among its other attractions.

There were free hot dogs, popcorn and candy, at the Home Show, which convinced young Cassius it was worth seeing, at least until he was dry and fed. The boys remained until seven in the evening, when the show closed. It was still raining heavily when they went outside, but when they returned to the place they had left the bike, it was gone.

Although Cash never beat his children, Cassius was afraid at facing his father's anger about the incident, so Cassius and Johnny searched the streets, looking for the bike. They had no success, and at last, they decided to go back to the gym, where it was known that the white boxing instructor was a policeman.

A police officer, Joe Martin took the report of the stolen bike, and as Cassius left the gym, Martin noticed Cassius' natural boxing stance in the way he carried himself and gave him an application to join a new program for youngsters who wanted to learn how to box. Cassius stuck the paper in his pocket and forgot about it when he went home to face the expected criticism of his father for the lost bicycle his mother had saved every extra dollar for.

Martin had a Saturday afternoon amateur boxing show on local TV called *Tomorrow's Champions.* That Saturday after the theft of his new bike, Cassius saw his friend the policeman/trainer on the show and remembered the application. He went to find the pants where he'd put the application, but the jeans had been washed. However, Bird had retrieved it from his pocket while she had been separating clothing to be washed.

Bird and Cash were a little uncertain about the idea of their son becoming a boxer, or even learning how to box for that matter. Of course Cash thought of ". . .the Clay face. . ." being beat around but, they decided anything in the way of organized athletics was better than having him run with a gang of boys during the volatile times of Civil Rights. They gave him their permission. With his parents' approval, Cassius ran all the way back to the gym.

Ali says he remembered jumping into the ring with an older boxer as soon as he reached the gym, and throwing wild punches that rarely hit their target. He was skinny, and had never before worn the gloves that would eventually be his ally in numerous victories.

After a minute in the ring, the outcome was as expected—a bloody nose for Clay.

However, he was not discouraged; and an

older boy advised him to stick with the other new fellows until he picked up some tricks of the trade. But Ali said later that there was really no one to teach him the proper method of fighting. Joe Martin taught him how to place his feet and throw a proper right cross, but the policeman knew little more about professional boxing.

Young Cassius continued to fight with great enthusiasm, if with little training, and Martin soon began to feature him on his show, *Tomorrow's Champions.* His first match was with a white boy, Ronny O'Keefe, and Cassius won by a split vote. Later, he said that he fought almost like a girl in those days, flailing around, and leaving himself open to blows.

His first "official" win gave him new recognition with his neighborhood street gang, which he had not completely abandoned despite his parents' hopes, and with his family as well. Each week Martin continued to book him on his show, primarily because Cassius would not give up, he'd continue trying to win, flailing away even when it was apparent he was exhausted. The other young fighters could not wear him down, and eventually they got discouraged and quit.

Cassius continued to win. And more importantly, each time he appeared on the TV show he got four dollars.

Joe Martin, who was Cassius' first trainer and worked with him from the age of twelve until he returned from Rome in the 1960 Olympic Games—with the gold—claimed that Cash Clay never came to see his son in any of his amateur fights. Martin says he certainly would have remembered Cash's presence, but he doesn't. Fred Stoner, Cassius' first black trainer at the Grace Community Center, says that Cash and Bird came to watch their son the first three months he trained with him, but stopped coming after that.

Ali denies these reports emphatically, saying that his parents only missed his out of town bouts. Regardless, it does seem that Cassius had the support of his parents in his choice of a professional boxing career.

As mentioned in the Ring Record, at the back of this book, there are varying claims as to the number of amateur bouts. Sources agree that he lost less than ten of his more than one-hundred amateur fights. However, Ali says that he learned more from one of his rare defeats than he did from his many wins.

Fighting in his first Kentucky State Golden Gloves match, he was beaten decisively by a black fighter who had received his training from Fred Stoner. Stoner had been working

During his exile from professional boxing, the media came to Ali's aid. In this "Battle of the Century" a computerized fight

that was staged to determine who would have won if Ali could have fought Rocky Marciano.

at the Grace Community Center gym, which was in a predominately black neighborhood, and catered to blacks for many years. Stoner's boys were better boxers than those who trained under Joe Martin. They were counterpunchers, with better timing and rhythm, and they were known for their quick jabs—a technique critical to Cassius' future style.

According to Ali, Joe Martin wouldn't use any of Stoner's fighters to fight his boys on his show for fear they'd make him look bad. In addition, Martin had a strict rule that his boys couldn't visit Stoner's gym and accept instruction from him. Most of Martin's fighters were white, while all of Stoner's were black.

But Stoner's boys continued to outfight all newcomers, and at last Cassius was impressed enough to leave Martin and join Stoner's group. He did not concern himself with the pettiness of the trainers and soon after introduced himself to Fred Stoner. Soon he was working out in the basement of the Center with the Stoner boys.

This make-shift gym lacked many of the amenities of the Center as a whole, and lacked many conveniences and the more elaborate equipment that Clay had been used to at Joe Martin's gym. But in those surroundings, Fred Stoner had shaped many a great black profes-

In his attempt to return to the boxing world, Muhammed Ali had to face many an untried boxer. Here, Ali is seen delivering a fifteenth round knockout blow to Chuck Wepner.

sional fighter.

Unlike Martin, Stoner observed what Martin was doing—and his show *Tomorrow's Champions*. Once Stoner had seen Cassius on *Tomorrow's Champions*, he admired the courage shown by the young fighter. He did, however, observe the obvious lack of training in Cassius' technique. After Cassius approached Stoner he was told that the boys at Grace Center trained from eight in the evening until midnight, and Cassius was required to be there every night.

The morning following his first meeting with Stoner, he was confronted by Joe Martin, telling him to make a choice. Well, the choice had already been made. But because he was on Martin's show, and needed the four dollars, he promised to stay away from Stoner.

By the end of his first year as an amateur fighter, Cassius knew that he wanted to become a professional. To succeed, he knew he'd have to make the transition to Stoner's group even if it meant losing the greatly needed money.

At the time, he put in four hours after school working for the Catholic Sisters at Nazareth College, across the street from the Columbia Gym. There, he cleaned and dusted and took care of the library.

From six to eight, he continued training with Joe Martin; and now he began doubling up, secretly attending Stoner's group as well. It was a demanding schedule, but it helped toughen him up.

Joe Martin remembered that Cassius even as a youngster was unpopular with the other fighters because he taunted them in the ring, a characteristic he would carry with him throughout his career. And, the fact he won so many of his fights, didn't help his popularity with the other fighters, either.

As Cassius made the transition to Stoner's ways of training he soon learned that Fred Stoner's religion of training was roadwork, and the discipline in his gym was unrelenting. His boys were made to shoot two-hundred left jabs without stopping, until they could perform this action without showing any strain. Then, he taught them the science of fighting, footwork, punching and movement, how to block and how to shoot right crosses, over and over again. When that was done, the boys did a hundred push-ups and a hundred deep knee bends.

Cassius Clay practiced everything Fred Stoner taught him, and then began to develop a style of his own. A composite, if you will of all the different training he had observed and received. He practiced pulling back from punches even when the professionals around the gym warned him that one of these days, he would get his head knocked off for doing so. But the wiser heads remembered that the famous black champion, Jack Johnson, The Big Black Fire, had also leaned back from time to time.

Older boxers watching Cassius in his amateur bouts thought he was an easy target. They were wrong. He developed a dodging mechanism—almost a sixth sense which protected him. It was as if this mechanism told him subliminally how far to duck at one time, and when he should move back, and when to make a crippling blow.

Both Joe Martin and Fred Stoner encouraged Cassius to aim for the U.S. Olympic Boxing Team. They told him the gold medal was worth a million dollars to the fighter who could win it.

But there was a lot of work ahead.

Cassius' first official win was as a flyweight novice in the Golden Gloves tournament in Louisville in 1954; he was still only twelve years old. His determination to be successful in boxing left little time for his studies. He wasn't a good student, for he was almost totally absorbed in boxing. Through his days at

DuVall Junior High School and throughout his years at Central High, most of his schoolwork was "ghosted" by his best friend Ronnie King, who was known as a good student around campus.

Cassius, Ronnie, and his younger brother Rudy still ran with the gangs together, fought in the streets together, went looking for girls together. They also tried boxing together, but Ronnie King quit doing that—constantly ending up with his nose bleeding.

Cassius Clay won six Golden Gloves tournaments in his home state, moving up the classes from light to welter, to middleclass, to light-heavy, and at last to heavyweight. It was very important for Cassius to work his way up to the heavyweight division. Because he knew as everyone else did it was the heavyweights who earned the fame—and the money.

In 1958 at the age of sixteen, he fought in the Tournament of Champions in Chicago. Actually, he should have been there a year earlier, but a doctor in Louisville discovered an irregularity in his heart and disqualified him for the event in 1957. The murmur cleared up, a temporary setback, never to return again.

The Tournament of Champions was divided between Chicago and New York, with half of the states sending their entries to each city.

The setting in Chicago was the humongous Chicago Stadium, where three boxing matches were staged at the same time. The winners in each class from the two cities then met for the national title.

1958 was not to be Cassius' year. He was defeated in a second round, knocked out by Kent Green.

He came back the following year, however, and as a light heavyweight, won both the national Golden Gloves title and the National Amateur Athletic Union tournament, held in Toledo, Ohio.

In 1960, he repeated his previous sweep of both tournaments. It was in this year also that his brother, Rudy, entered in the AAU tournament as a light heavyweight. Still being technically a light heavyweight himself, Cassius fought in the tournament as a heavyweight, until Rudy was defeated. Then, he returned to his regular weight division— he refused the possibility of facing his brother in the ring.

As AAU Champion, he won the right to participate in the Olympic trials, which would be held at the Cow Palace in San Francisco, California. There were becoming fewer and fewer goals left to attain in his amateur career.

Cassius was only eighteen when he traveled

to San Francisco for the Olympic trials, but he was by far the most publicized fighter who participated. And, the publicity was not all good. He mouthed off to the press whenever he had the chance and they didn't like it one bit. When he entered the ring for the second round elimination, he was jeered by many of the fans. To make matters worse, the newspapers criticized him for being a braggart in a tournament, which was supposed to be clean, pure, and "decent."

When it came time for the semi-final fight, Joe Martin threatened to remove him from the event if he didn't shut his mouth.

Cassius' final opponent in the trials was Army Champion Allen Hudson. To Clay, it was as though Uncle Sam had sent his representative. Hudson was a tall, slim black man described by Joe Torres as having a murderous left hand. In the first round, Cassius was knocked down by that left—he never saw it coming. The second round was even, but Cassius was in danger of losing the round and the fight until the third round, he landed a right cross, a damaging blow, to Hudson's jaw.

Hudson's legs buckled slightly. Seeing his opportunity, Cassius unleashed a furious barrage that forced the referee to stop the match. Hudson, regaining his composure, protested, but Cassius Clay would now be representing the United States of America in the 1960 Olympic Games in Rome, Italy.

First, however, he returned to Louisville to finish his last year of high school. Although he was the number one amateur boxer in his weight class in the country, Cassius Clay graduated in the bottom tenth of his class, actually receiving a certificate of attendance rather than a diploma.

The U.S. Olympic Boxing Team left for Rome, Italy in the middle of that summer, 1960. Because of an illness in his family, Joe Martin was unable to travel with young Cassius. It marked the first time he had not been in his most famous protege's corner.

Cassius' behavior abroad was no different than in the States—or anywhere else for that matter. He felt that to win attention, he would have to stir up the crowd. Yelling, jeering, taunting, and bragging about how he predicted his victories and eventually the gold medal brought photographers from all over the globe, which pushed other American contenders into the background. For that, he was unpopular with his own teammates, but received the attention he so greatly craved.

Cassius' first fight was against Belgium's Yvon Becaus. Becaus could not absorb the

American's combination jabs, and was stopped in the second round.

His next opponent was the USSR's Gennadily Shatkov, who was a far more experienced fighter. The fight was less than exciting, but in the end, Cassius managed to outjab the Russian and won on his own mastery of the skill of boxing.

Jose' Torres thought that if the fight had gone any longer than six rounds, Cassius could have been in serious trouble because of the Russian's shear strength, but in amateur competition, there are either five two-minute or three three-minute rounds, and this format helped young Cassius by keeping the fighting time limited.

Defeating the Soviet gave Cassius new confidence in his next bouts. He would face the Australian Tony Madigan next. He had previously faced Madigan in the National Golden Gloves the year before, and while this fight was hard fought, it wasn't even close. Cassius won a unanimous decision.

In the finals, Cassius faced Poland's Champion Zbigniew "Ziggy" Piertrzkowkski. He was a veteran of over two-hundred fights and had won the bronze medal for Poland just four years before in the 1956 Olympic Games. Also, he was a lefty, which always proved to be an

October 2, 1980 Ali met Larry Holmes in the ring in Las Vegas, Nevada. Holmes won the match in two rounds. After

the bout Ali said that he was shaky because of the increased dosage of Thyrolar he was recently given.

irritation to Cassius, due to the unconventional stance the lefties used.

The Pole, similarly, respected Cassius' growing reputation. They met in the ring. Cassius quickly adjusted to the opponent's lefty stance, thrusting two quick jolt to the Pole's face. Blood spurted from Piertrzkowkski's face, and the Pole literally ran around the ring to avoid the fight from being stopped. At the final bell, the Pole was up against the ropes, blood oozing from his nose, mouth and both eyes. This fight was later known as the ". . . bloodiest in recent Olympic memory."

Soon after, Cassius heard the national anthem of the country he represented and received the gold medal. That night he wore the medal to bed in his last days in Rome. He was now "The Greatest" or so he thought, and he had proved to the world that it was so.

Cassius returned to the States, and when he got to New York he could be seen still wearing his gold medal. Joe Martin met him at Idlewild Airport. There was only one way for him to go now, Martin suggested, professional.

There had been a strong interest in sponsoring a professional career for Cassius. In particular, there was interest shown to Joe Martin from an acquaintance, William Reynolds, heir to the R.J. Reynolds Tobacco

Company. And, Joe was very interested in having a lucrative managing career with Cassius. So on Reynolds' direction, he put Cassius up in his private suite in New York's luxurious Waldorf-Astoria Hotel. Cassius, still wearing his gold medal, relaxed and enjoyed the luxury the hotel had to offer while the two men discussed his future.

Reynolds offered a contract and picked up all acquired expenses including extravagant gifts for Clay's family. After these preliminary business meetings, Cassius and Martin flew home to Louisville, greeted by a phenomenally enthusiastic crowd.

Cassius was greeted as a conquering hero by a mixed crowd of blacks and whites. He was given a motorcade parade through the streets of the city, escorted by every spare police car in Louisville. The motorcade stopped at Central High, where Cassius was greeted by hundreds of students carrying banners reading "Welcome Home Cassius Clay."

Even before Cassius went to Europe, he was given a summer job on William Reynolds' estate as a houseboy. Because of racial tension that existed—no matter the business relationship—the millionaire made it impossible for Cassius to approach him on a personal level. Also, he found it very difficult to even directly communicate in any way with the man who wanted to support his career. These facts stirred second thoughts in Cassius about affiliating with Reynolds, who he considered a racist.

Although messages would go back and forth through Martin, this obvious lack of trust between Reynolds and Clay troubled Cassius, and would lead to an eventual parting of the ways for the two.

Clay had always resented the treatment shown to him by Reynolds while these negotiations were going on, for although Reynolds had encouraged Cassius to win the gold medal, and that it would be "worth a million," he never let Clay forget that he was of a lower societal stature—having Cassius eat his meals on the back porch of the estate along with the family pets and so on. It was surely for his trust in Martin, Cassius didn't re-evaluate his situation sooner.

And there were other embarrassing incidents.

One hot afternoon, Mrs. Reynolds' black Cadillac Fleetwood blocked the driveway to the main home. Cassius got into the car to put it into the garage. The heat was sweltering, so Cassius turned on the air conditioner, then sat back to enjoy the cool air—and the luxurious automobile.

Next thing he heard someone screaming for help. Cassius thought a thief was on the compound. He slammed on the brakes and jumped out of the car to defend the estate. As he turned to face the house he saw Reynolds' aunt marching towards him shouting, "Nigger, how dare you; get out of that car."

Later, when Cassius finally did receive the offered contract he had been so patient in waiting for, he turned it down, although his father wanted him to accept it. He couldn't see himself working, at any price, for someone who was obviously a racist.

Joe Martin later blamed Clay for turning down the contract, claiming that he had psychological problems with white authority. But he was wrong, because instead, Cassius accepted a contract offered by a group of white Louisville millionaires headed up by Bill Faversham.

The contract was to run until 1966, with the Louisville group earning fifty percent of all Cassius' earnings. Along with this came a ten thousand dollar cash advance on the deal, which Cassius used to pay off the mortgage on his parents' home—and fix the leaks that had forever haunted them, and rebuild the dilapidated porch.

*In this return match held in the Superdome in New Orleans on
September 19, 1978, Ali attempts to reclaim the title from*

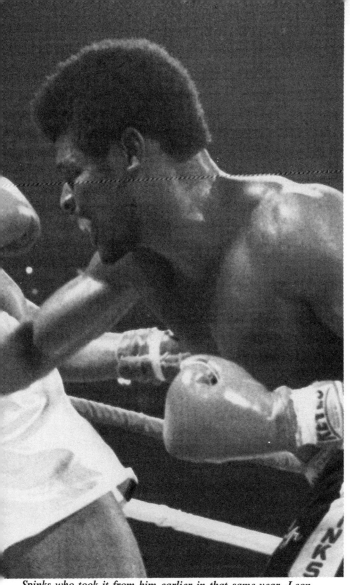

*Spinks who took it from him earlier in that same year. Leon
Spinks lost and Ali was again the Heavyweight Champion.*

Cassius was proud of the contract and himself, and he carried the list of his sponsors for several months in his shirt pockets just as before he had displayed the Olympic gold medal he had won.

He had both with him when he and Ronnie King rode their motorbikes downtown for a visit with the Mayor of Louisville.

Returning home after a full day, it began to rain. Cassius stopped at a newly remodeled restaurant, despite Ronnie's protests of not wanting to be late getting home. A motorcycle gang was dining in the restaurant. One, called Kentucky Slim, Cassius had seen attending his matches.

Cassius wasn't naive enough to think that his gold medal would give him entrance anywhere, but he did think it would give him some clout in his hometown. But the ugly head of racism reared, and the owner refused he and Ronnie service. He displayed his medal and explained who he was. The owner still refused.

The leader of the motorcycle gang, "Frog," observed the entire scene. Ronnie tried to buffer the increasingly tense situation, but it was of no avail.

As they left the restaurant, they were followed by Frog and the gang. Kentucky Slim

Muhammad Ali wasn't just a boxer, he became a world
celebrity. Here he is shown with Lola Falana. They attend a
dinner held in the Champion's honor.

circled around on his bike, then came back to tell Cassius that Frog wanted his gold medal to give his girlfriend.

Cassius was outraged, but controlled himself. He realized he had acted immaturely, and it would be worth it just to avoid a violent confrontation.

He knew this gang was known to have chain whipped a number of black youths in the area, so without answering the request the two speed away on their motorcycles, in an effort to out run the pursuing gang.

Cassius thought he could give Frog and his gang the slip by cutting over to the Jefferson County Bridge. They did lose them, for a time, but when they reached the ramp to the bridge itself, Frog and the gang were there to meet them. The motorbikes the black youths had, were no match for the cycles the gang had— and they knew it.

Frog wanted Cassius; he rode right by Ronnie to reach him. Timing his act perfectly, like some choreographed dance of death, Ronnie jumped off his bike, throwing it under the front wheel of Frog's attacking vehicle.

Frog saw Ronnie's action too late and cut to the left, smashing himself and his girlfriend, who was riding shotgun, into the bridgerail.

Kentucky Slim came up and whipped his

chain at Cassius. Cassius caught it with his quick hand, and jerked Slim off his bike, smashing his fist into Slim's jaw as the now prostrate Slim lay on the cold damp ground. Ronnie, by now holding a switchblade on Frog, yelled for the group to retreat. On Frog's command and with his girlfriend crying hysterically, the bikers broke up.

Frog, Slim, and his girlfriend moved away, humiliated.

But to Cassius, now the gold medal had lost its magic. Hell, he thought, it wasn't even made of real gold. It really meant nothing because a black man had won it. He was no better off in society as he had been before.

Thinking on this he jerked the red, white and blue ribbon, which held the medal in place about his muscular neck, and with all his might hurled it into the deepest part of the Ohio River.

In disgust, he turned away, knowing that the medal only proved he was the best in amateur boxing, and boxing alone—he was not "the best." He had won it for himself and not for the principles of a racist America he was beginning to know so well.

Chapter Four

The Young Olympian

WHEN CASSIUS CLAY RETURNED from Rome with the Olympic gold medal, he was bombarded with offers from managers in the professional boxing league. Rocky Marciano sent him a telegraph stating: "You have the promise. I can give you the guidance." Archie Moore wired, similarly: "If you desire to have an excellent manager call me collect." There were talks with Cus D'Amato, one of the most respected managers in the business, who then handled Floyd Patterson, the current "champ," and calls from others as well.

The Olympic champion's own first choice

I Am The Greatest: the Adventures of Muhammad Ali *became a hit with the Saturday childrens'lineup for NBC. Seen here going over the script, Ali gets ready to do the voice over.*

would have been Joe Louis. But Louis was from a different era of boxing. He was a quiet man, disliking the outrageous style of Clay. Because of Clay's bragging, Louis issued a statement saying that he predicted Clay would lose every contest he had. Cassius then offered the position to Sugar Ray Robinson, searching him out in New York. Robinson, nearing the end of his own illustrious career, was too busy to be bothered. He brushed Clay off, telling him to come see him in a couple of years.

But patience wasn't one of Clay's long suits.

Before signing his contract with the Louisville Eleven, Cassius had already signed for his first professional bout with Tunny Hunsaker, a white fighter from Fayetteville, West Virginia. The date was October 29, 1960, and the fight was heavily promoted by famed Louisville boxing promoter Bill King. A large crowd turned out to see the Olympic champion in his first pro fight. He still wore his Olympic boxing trunks with "USA" emblazoned on the leg.

It was not an awe-inspiring fight. Cassius admitted later that he had been over confident, careless, having eaten dinner only one hour before the bout. He paid for that mistake when Hunsaker hit him in the stomach so hard that he nearly expelled. He came back, though, to

A training photo from 1971. Although Ali wanted to go right for Frazier and the championship, Frazier and the WBA made it difficult for him because of his three-year suspension. Ali settled to fight Jerry Quarry, the second ranked boxer.

finish the full six rounds and win by a decision. Cassius' share of the purse was two-thousand dollars.

His second fight against Herb Siler fought in Miami Beach on December 27 of that same year, brought him only two hundred dollars. It was not until his sixth fight, that he again won more than a thousand dollars—in fact it was $2,548.

In the meantime, his choice of manager had narrowed down to Archie Moore and Angelo Dundee. After the lackluster performances against Hunsaker and Siler, the Louisville Millionaires decided to send him to Moore's training camp near San Diego, California.

The camp was in the country, twenty-five miles from the city of San Diego, and could be reached only by a long winding dirt road. Moore had painted the names of the immortals of boxing on boulders surrounding the encampment. Some of them included: Jack Johnson, Rocky Marciano, Sugar Ray Robinson, and Joe Louis. Later in his life when Clay finally built his own camp in the Pocono Mountains of Pennsylvania he also had boulders trucked in from the Southwest and did the same thing.

Archie Moore's first move was to challenge Clay to a run up the hill to his gym. Clay led the way for the first half mile or so, then he ran out of wind. Moore quickly caught up, without much effort, and easily passed the winded Cassius.

Cassius didn't want to do the road work and was anxious to begin sparring, but Moore believed discipline and that the art of pacing yourself were the first things the young fighter had to learn. He gave Clay a list of chores to do about the gym, things he had to do before he was allowed to spar, and continued to put Clay off when he asked to be put in the ring. Moore simply told him that in four years he'd be ready.

One day Clay, still prodding Moore to be able to practice in the ring, did get into the ring with his manager. This was Cassius' chance to take out his frustrations for the weeks of working doing menial tasks, and for being so isolated. This was his chance to fight.

A week later he left Archie Moore's training camp for good. When he got home, Bill Faversham, of the Louisville group called Dundee at his Fifth Street Gym in Miami Beach.

Clay had already introduced himself to Dundee the year before in Louisville, where Dundee had brought Willie Pastrano to fight Johnny Holman at Freedom Hall in downtown

Louisville. They had met when Angelo got a phone call from Cassius in the hotel lobby that he was staying.

Dundee later recalls the young Clay as having said on their first meeting: "My name is Cassius Marcellus Clay, Jr. I have won six Golden Gloves tournaments in Kentucky. I have fought in the Tournament of Champions in Chicago. I won the National Amateur Athletic Union Championship in Toledo, and I am the 1959 National Golden Gloves light heavyweight champion. And I'm going to win the Gold medal in Rome."

Now, Angelo told Pastrano there was a crazy man downstairs who was insisting on meeting him. The older fighter, looking at television, thought to himself there wasn't anything good to watch, so he allowed Clay to come up. It was even more strange, because following behind Cassius was his brother, Rudy, carrying a plaster cast of his brother and a full-size portrait of the future champion.

Cassius spent over three hours with Dundee and Pastrano, telling them about the fighters he had easily defeated and asking questions. Cassius wanted to know everything about boxing. Under their direction, he bought every book available on boxing and read every one of them.

Following that meeting, Cassius met them a second time in the gym, where Clay was allowed to spar two rounds. Pastrano was then the third ranked light heavyweight in the world, later he won the title.

In *The Greatest,* Cassius recalls the sparring round with Pastrano. Willie was fast, but Clay was faster, and his jab was smoother—and his reach was extraordinary. He was able to easily jab Pastrano, unscathed, and ended up stopping the fight so as not to hurt his friend.

It was early that winter after Cassius left Moore's direction when Bill Faversham called Dundee in Miami. Angelo told him to send Clay down after Christmas Day, but Faversham said Cassius was anxious to have a match before the Christmas holiday.

So young Clay came down to Miami by train. Angelo met him at the station and took him to the Smith Hotel in downtown Miami, where he had arranged for a living situation with a young fighter from the Caribbean. Cassius was anxious to fight from the moment he stepped off the train, and his manager found it hard to restrain Clay's volatile temperament.

The desired fight before Christmas Day didn't happen, but Dundee got Clay a preliminary bout before the Willie Pastrano-

*Cassius Clay poses here with former Heavyweight Champion,
Joe Louis at Madison Square Garden before the Clay-Folley*

match. Said Clay, *"I wish you were twenty years younger, and we'd see then who is the greatest."*

Jesse Bowdry main event on the 27th of the month. He was to meet Siler, and eventually stopped him with a fourth round TKO Jose' Torres wrote up the match, saying:

"A right to the midsection and a left hook to the jaw."

Clay walked out that night, just after his first bout saying, "I'm gonna be the heavyweight champion of the world."

Dundee's older brother, Chris, promoted the following three fights for Clay. They were to be held in the same arena. All were won by decisive knockouts. On January 17, Clay's birthday, he met Tony Esperti and knocked him out in three rounds. On February 7, 1961 in the pretrial to the National Boxing Association's Light Heavyweight Championships, he knocked out Jim Robinson in two minutes flat. Later that same month, he met Donnie Fleeman and defeated him in the seventh round.

Fleeman was a little tougher for Clay. He had had forty-five victories and twenty knockouts in fifty-one fights. It was also the first time Cassius was forced to go beyond six rounds, and the fight would probably have lasted the full eight rounds if Clay hadn't opened up cuts over both Fleeman's eyes—the blood gushing out of the cuts made it impossible for him to see, and the fight was ended.

The experience that winter was good for Clay; Cassius had learned that a professional just cannot fall like a house of cards with the first good blow. He began realizing he'd have to improve his fighting techniques on all levels. He learned that a professional had to shake off good jabs from his opponent, and not get hurt. Clay began to learn this—he was becoming a professional.

His sixth fight was against Lamar Clark. It would be in Louisville on April 29th. Clark was also an experienced fighter with over forty knockouts to his credit. Clay told the press, though, that he'd stop Clark in two rounds. His prediction came true—Clark went down late in the second round.

Clay would continue to make such predictions throughout his career; and most of them would be correct. In *The Greatest,* Clay tells Torres how these "premonitions" got started. He quotes Clay as saying:

"I began predicting the outcome of my fights after watching 'Gorgeous' George, the great wrestler. I hear this white fellow say, 'I am the world's greatest wrestler. I cannot be defeated. I am the greatest I am the King. If that sucker messes up my pretty waves in my hair, I'm gonna kill him. If that sucker whups me, I'm gonna get the next jet to Russia. I cannot be defeated. I am the prettiest; I am the greatest!' When he was in the ring, everybody just booed. I mean everybody. And I was mad, too. And I looked around and I saw everybody and they were mad.

"I saw fifteen-thousand people coming to see this man get beat. And this talking did it. And, I said, that is a g-o-o-o-o-o-o-d idea—I think I'll try that."

Clay's seventh fight was against The Hawaiian Giant, Kolo "Duke" Sabedong. The towering fighter had won fifteen out of twenty-seven bouts. The match was Clay's first ten-rounder, and was fought in Las Vegas, Nevada.

Although Sabedong was like a Goliath to Clay, it wasn't the fight Clay feared, it was the flight to Vegas that bothered him. He had always been afraid of flying and as an amateur, he pawned his gold watch to pay for a train ticket from San Francisco to Louisville in order to avoid a plane ride. He had wanted to take a cruise ship to Europe for the Olympics, but Joe Martin forced him to endure the flight. It is odd, but several great champions were and are afraid of air travel.

If he were to be able to meet his increasing schedule, it was a fear he would have to overcome. Dundee refused to let him take a train

A still from a.k.a. Cassius Clay *a feature film made for United Artists. The film followed the Champ's life from childhood through his dazzling career; a career that continued long after the film screened.*

to Las Vegas—and it seemed to effect the fight. Although Clay won the bout, it was by a close decision. Cassius was just unable to get a clean series of shots to the Hawaiian to score.

His fear of flight was one he did overcome later in his career. He even bought his own jet, eventually, and when he did have to take a commercial flight, he was often invited to the cockpit where he'd spend much of the flight with the captain and crew.

Clay's next three fights were back home in Louisville. The first of the three to be against ranked heavyweight, Alonzo Johnson. This would be the first time he met a ranked heavyweight in the ring.

The fight lasted ten rounds, a long match for Clay, but eventually the judgment was in his favor. He next faced Alex Miteff, predicting his opponent would go down in six. When this did happen, Clay turned to the audience, shouting, "I am the king; I am the greatest. Nobody will stop me—they'll all fall to me."

However, there would be another fight in Louisville. This time against Willie Besmanoff, a German. Clay predicted that he'd beat the German in seven rounds—a prediction that would force Cassius to prolong the fight for several rounds, dancing around the ring, so that his prediction would come true. And that it did.

Now, Dundee thought, Clay was ready for bigger things. No more small time for Cassius—he'd proven himself in the small time already. It was time for Clay to start fighting some validated fighters—some reputable fighters.

It was time to go to New York.

Chapter Five

The Greatest Goes Abroad

FIGHTERS CONSIDER MADISON SQUARE Garden in New York City as the pinnacle—the Taj Mahal of professional boxing. Angelo accepted a bid for Clay to fight Sonny Banks who was earning himself a name in the Detroit inner-city area. But it was Cassius, not Banks, who made the papers. He made another confident prediction before the fight began. Clay shouted: "The man must fall in the round I call—Banks must fall in four."

The audience erupted in applause. In the third round of the match, it looked as though the prediction would fail. Banks recovered

In a.k.a. Cassius Clay Muhammad Ali played himself. Here, he is shown as a young struggling boxer, showing off at one of the training centers at the start of his career.

from a series of blows and exacted a sharp left hook to Clay's jaw and Cassius went down. But Cassius came back with a fervor. In the next round, as predicted, Clay hit Banks with a combination that put him to the floor—the fight was over.

Although Clay won the match, Dundee was worried about Cassius' fall to the floor. He thought that a change of scenery would be good for Cassius and set up a match to be held in Miami Beach twelve days later. This time it was an easy win for Clay. He again carried the fight until the predicted round, and then knocked Warner to the canvas. This would be something he'd do time and time again.

Los Angeles was next on the itinerary. On April 23, 1962, he met George Logan in the ring. This time Dundee took Clay back to New York for a fight against an up-coming fighter named Billy Daniels. Daniels was a tough opponent, but like others before him, Clay was able to open up cuts to Daniels' face and the fight was stopped.

Back in Los Angeles, Clay met Alejandro Lavorante who fell in five rounds as predicted. The purse was a whopping $15,149, by far the largest amount for Clay to date. But that would seem like peanuts, as his next match would earn him three times that amount—

against Archie Moore.

Clay had finally hit the big time. There would be no more turning back. His destiny was wrought in professional boxing. Famous West Coast promoter, Ailene Eaton, jumped into the whirlwind Clay had created. He set up a match for Cassius, one that would be televised on pay closed-circuit TV.

Two weeks for the scheduled fight, sales for the closed-circuit theaters, a predecessor to cable TV, hadn't reached the break-even point, so the fight was rescheduled three weeks later. Cassius and Moore had already been exchanging insults to each other and the press, and Archie was quoted saying: "You mean another three weeks of listening to this guy shooting his big mouth off? Well, good, because I'm going to develop the 'lip-buttoner punch,' especially designed and created for that fresh boy."

Clay responded by writing a poem to the effect:

Archie had been living off the fat of the land
I'm here to give him his pension plan.
When you come to the fight, don't block aisle or door,
'Cause ya all going home after round

four.

Moore was an older fighter, having spent twenty-five years as a professional. His head was grizzled. It was nearly an embarrassment when he showed up to the fight with elastic support trunks that came up to his nipples, to cover his middle-aged paunch. Moore told the press he was forty-three—but boxing insiders knew he was more like fifty.

Cassius let Moore chase him about the ring to tire the older man out for about two rounds. Then at the end of the second round Clay made a jab to Moore's jaw. The crack of the blow made the crowd cheer. Clay became more aggressive, and in successive rounds pummeled the now-dazed Moore so ferociously that the fight was stopped in the fourth round.

This was the first non-championship bout featuring professional boxers since the fight between "Irish" Bob Murphy and the Raging Bull, Jake LaMotta twelve years before.

While Clay was busy with Moore, there was a match between Sonny Liston and Floyd Patterson at Madison Square Gardens in New York for the championship. Patterson, having lost to Liston, awaited a rematch to regain his championship position, and turned down a fight with Cassius. But Clay was just as unen-

Muhammad Ali embraces actor, Johnny Sekka, who plays the leading role, Bilal, in the film Mohammad, Messenger of God. *Ali, shown here at a screening of the film has always supported the Muslim cause since his conversion.*

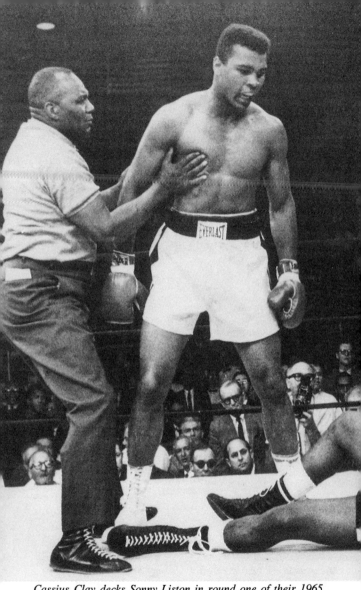

*Cassius Clay decks Sonny Liston in round one of their 1965
rematch for the World Heavyweight Title which Clay, of course
won. This historic encounter is one of the memorable bouts*

spotlighted in the HBO Sports special Boxing's Greatest Knockouts. *The event was co-hosted by then current champion, Mike Tyson.*

thusiastic about fighting Patterson as Patterson was in fighting Clay. He wanted to go straight to Liston; he felt it was time for him to be "the champ."

A massive publicity campaign for the bout was launched. Dundee and Faversham were excited about the proposed match. For the first time, the press began to take Clay as a serious contender. With his style, and mouth, he had restored glamour and prestige to the waning art of boxing.

There was demand to see Liston meet Patterson for a second time and Liston wanted to grant Patterson the rematch.

In the mean time to keep money coming in and to keep Clay in practice, Dundee set up a fight in Pittsburgh, Pennsylvania, against ex-San Francisco Forty-Niner, Charlie Powell. Cassius predicted three rounds; in round three Powell was down.

Next he would face Doug Jones, ranked number two in the standings. And, although New York was dealing with newspaper strike ninety-five days old, the match sold out. Not only had Clay become a celebrity, but it was also the first time in thirteen years that the Garden had sold out for a boxing event. Clay wrote a poem to commemorate the event:

Jones like to mix.

So I'll let it go to six.
If he talks jive,
I'll cut it to five.
And if he talks some more,
I'll cut it to four.

Cassius had done a very smart thing in this—it gave him three rounds in order to beat his opponent, a prediction which would be easier to fulfill if he ran into any trouble.

Jones was a fleshy 188 pounds at weigh-in, and looked a little overweight. Although the odds had stayed in Clay's favor, they dropped from 4-1, to 2-1—bookies thought, because of Jones' hard-hitting style it would be a close fight.

Just as the fight was to start, Clay turned to Jones and shouted, "Hey, how tall are you?"

Jones replied, "Why do you want to know?"

"So I'll know how far to step back when I knock you out in the fourth," said Clay, grinning.

But Clay would fail in his attempt to predict the outcome of the fight. After twelve correct predictions, it was another close bout. In ten rounds, two of the judges scored four for Jones, six for Clay and the third scored them as even. The fight would become controversial. Many of the boxing elite thought Jones was the victor. In fact, the Associated Press scored the fight against Cassius. The fight had become an embarrassment for Clay. In fact, Jones received a thunderous ovation from the crowd as he left the ring. Jones would be recorded in boxing history as one of the toughest fighters ever.

Despite this setback, offers for fights continued to pour in. One being a rematch with Jones. There was also a proposition from the Garden for a match with ex-heavyweight champion Ingemar Johannson. But this was not to be. The Millionaires decided to send Cassius to England for a bout with top-ranked Henry Cooper. Cooper was an experienced fighter, but his career had begun to wane. Even though he was twenty-nine years old, he was considered by some as a "has been." His reputation as a fighter was good, and he was known for two things: his ability to down an opponent with one blow—and as a bleeder.

By this time Clay had met Drew "Bundini" Brown, a man Clay would know throughout his future career. Brown was the only man known who could out belt Cassius, and it was said that between the two of them they could overwhelm the opposition with their voices.

Clay had already established himself as a fighter in Europe, having won the gold medal in Rome, 1960. In England he was known, but not popular with the conservative English populace. He issued a statement to the press about the up-coming bout with Cooper, "Henry Cooper will think he's Gordon Cooper when I put him in orbit." Gordon Cooper being the American astronaut. The English audience didn't take kindly Cassius' boasting.

The promoter for the bout in England was a man named Jack Solomon. The night before the match, Cassius announced that he was the un-crowned king of heavyweight champions. Solomon, picking up on the comment, had a crown and royal-type robe made, which Clay wore to his weigh-in. This was considered a staged act and in poor taste to the British people.

Some thought it was a mockery to the House of Windsor, the Royal Family, admired by many of the people of England, and respected by most who lived in Western Europe.

Cooper weighed in at just over 185 pounds, Clay was at 207. Clay was dressed flamboyantly, wearing white satin bath robe which had "Cassius The Greatest" on the back. He was pushing his luck with the conservative crowd, for under British rules the referee was the sole decider of the match—personal feelings could easily dictate the decision if it were a close match.

Considered to be a slow starter, Cooper surprised his audience by coming out fast. This brought a standing ovation from the biased crowd. And—the round ended in Clay's nose being bloodied. This made the English crowd go wild. Shouts of "Beat that Yank" were heard throughout the arena.

The second round was all Clay's, though. He came out at the bell aggressively, intending to knock out the Englishman in the fifth round. He jabbed at Cooper's weak spots—the eyes, ears and nose. By the fourth, Cassius had Cooper cornered and bleeding from cuts around both his eyes. But the tide turned again when, at the conclusion of the fourth round, Clay became cornered himself and was taken down by an unseen left hook. The bell rang with Clay attempting to get to his feet, and Cooper's face completely covered with blood.

Dundee managed to extend the one-minute rest period by spotting a rip in one of the gloves worn by Clay. Some say he forcibly enlarged the tear, so that by the boxing rules he could demand a new pair of gloves to be brought in. This was legal under the rules, and more importantly, gave Clay a chance to clear his head.

In the next round Clay charged Cooper wildly, jabbing at his head with two rights, as the crowd began to throw paper wads into the ring. Cooper was now blinded by blood, obviously hurt, and the referee stopped the fight.

Cassius won the bout, but later admitted that Cooper had hit him harder than any man had ever before.

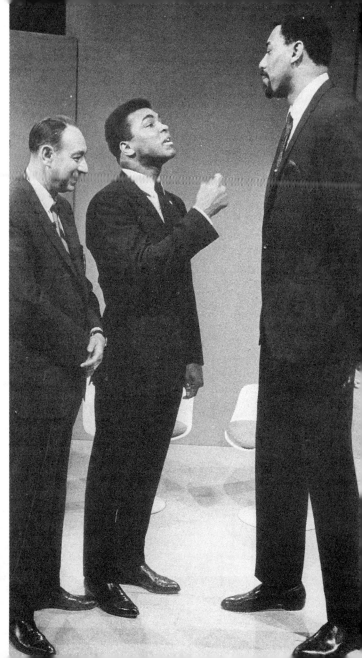

Chapter Six

The
Greatest

BY THE END 1963 CLAY FELT IT was time for Sonny Liston and the title.

Clay had challenged Liston for some time now. And as a stunt, had even climbed into the ring with Liston after the second Liston-Patterson bout. The media had a field day proclaiming the match the greatest grudge fight in the history of the sport. The event would be eventually set for February 25, 1964 in Miami, Florida.

On to Denver, Colorado. Flagged by his closest friends, Rudy, Ronnie King, and black comedian, Clay Tyson, Clay arrived in the Mile-

As a commentor for ABC Wide World Of Sports, *Ali met with greats such as basketball star Wilt "The Stilt" Chamberlain. Here they are shown with host, Howard Cosell.*

High City. The "boys" having arrived, called the local newspapers disguising their voices saying, "Cassius Clay has arrived at Sonny Liston's house and is getting ready to break in."

Nearing Liston's house, police sirens were heard in the distance. Clay blew the horn on the bus while famed photographer Howard Binghan banged on the door and yelled for Liston to come out. The neighbors craned their heads from their doors and windows to see the show.

Liston emerged from his house carrying a iron fireplace poker. Cassius, realizing the stunt had gone too far, locked the door on the bus just as Liston speared a window, shattering glass to the pavement. The police had had enough—the confrontation was broken up and Liston returned to his home.

Just as Clay began to drive away, he turned to his adversary and yelled, "You big, ugly bear! The policeman and those dogs saved you. You're no champ. You're a chump. You're gonna fall in eight 'cause I'm the greatest!"

The incident headlined the papers. Clay knew it would. He also knew that people would come to see the fight just to see Liston shut his mouth. But this fight almost never happened.

But the match went on and was fought as scheduled on February 25, 1964.

Liston was confident, having never being forced to fight more than six rounds. But as the fourth round took place, he knew Clay was a different contender. He threw a desperation blow, that missed its target, leaving open the victory for Clay.

And Clay had another agenda running at the time.

Three days before the match, Dundee burst into Clay's dressing room in shock.

"You know who's out there?" He opened the door. And standing outside in the hall was the controversial, yet world famous Black Muslim, Malcolm X. "You know what will happen if the newspapers pick that up? They'll denounce you. They'll wreck the fight." Angelo continued, "We got to get him outta here. If the newspapers make the association, we're finished."

Dundee didn't know one thing: Clay had already joined the religious group that Malcolm X was a prominent member of, The Nation of Islam. He was no longer Cassius Clay, he was Cassius X.

Shortly thereafter he was given the name Muhammad Ali from Elijah Muhammad leader of his new faith.

From the beginning of his career, Clay had sensed that the crowds came to see a disliked, or at least controversial man defeated. Always the showman, he capitalized on this intense relationship with the public; and now it came back in a way he had never imagined—to possibly overpower him.

Two months after Ali eventually won the Liston match becoming the Heavyweight Champion, the World Boxing Association stripped Ali of his newly won championship status on the flimsy grounds that he had promised to give Liston a rematch and had reneged on the agreement. When Liston previously won the title from Floyd Patterson, there was the same understanding; that time the WBA made noise, but did absolutely nothing to impair Liston's career.

Others, however, wanted to see the two meet again; and the match was sanctioned by New York, California, Massachusetts and all of Western Europe. The match was set up to go in Tokyo, but was again prevented, when even a temporary passport was denied by the U.S. State Department.

But there was still happiness for Ali. After resting a while from the first Liston fight, Ali married his first wife, Sonji Roi; and in that same year, 1964, he took her on a tour through

Here is a rare photo of Muhammad Ali and two of his children from his marriage to Belinda Boyd. It is known that he loved his children very much and kept them out of the media eye.

Africa where he was hailed as a continental hero. He met the heads of state, including Gamal Abdel Nasser of Egypt and Kwame Nkrumah of Ghana, all of whom congratulated him for being the first Muslim to win a world championship in any sport.

The return Liston match was scheduled for October, 1964 in Boston; but three days before the fight, Ali suffered a hernia and was hospitalized. Intense pressure was put on the promoter, Sam Silverman, mostly by those critical of Ali, and the fight was quickly stifled. Silverman was reported to have lost fifty-thousand dollars in the ill-fated turn of events.

Ali's sponsors, the eleven white millionaires from his hometown of Louisville—the Louisville Millionaire Club—who had given him his first professional contract, began frantic efforts to find a new promoter and location. At last they settled on an obscure town in the state of Maine, Lewiston. The fight was on again, and Ali began to train as hard as ever. And on May 25, 1965, fifteen months to the day after winning the title from Liston, the two met in the ring for a second time.

Ali, although he had been close to Malcolm X, kept his ties close with the Nation of Islam, while the latter had broken away with his own following.

When Malcolm X was killed earlier this same year just before the second Liston fight, rumors circulated that some of Malcolm X's supporters were plotting to kill Ali, now the most famous Black Muslim, to revenge the death of their fallen leader. The rumor stated that two carloads of triggermen were supposedly on their way to kill him, either in training camp or when he entered the ring.

Ali tried to ignore the rumors and train on. But when five Government Agents came to his hotel to tell him that they had been ordered to post a twenty-four hour guard outside his door, he knew there was more to worry about than just blatant rumors. A police escort began accompanying him to the training camp each morning, and before he was allowed to use the training track for road work, five policemen checked the field closely. As he ran, he saw other policemen, armed with rifles, every five or six-hundred feet.

Three days before the fight, during a sparring match, Jimmy Ellis landed a sharp right cross on Ali's rib, bruising the ribs that had already been the Champ's Achilles' Heal. He didn't tell the doctors just how bad they hurt, afraid the fight would be postponed again or even canceled. But this fight seemed to be jinxed. That night he had a discussion with Sonji,

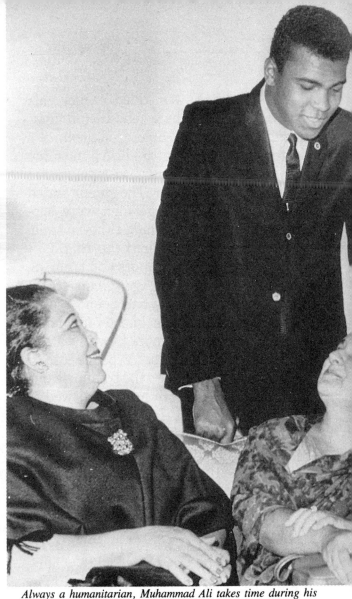

Always a humanitarian, Muhammad Ali takes time during his tour of West Africa to meet the Ahmed family from Dacca,

Pakistan. Standing with him is his father Cash, sitting with their hosts is his mother "Bird" Clay.

who told him she couldn't follow some of the stricter rules of their faith as he demanded. Because of this they agreed to separate. Three years later by early 1967 they were legally divorced.

The marriage had been dissembling because of Sonji's objections to Islam, and by the time of the second Liston bout much of the emotion was gone—it just seemed to be a parting of the ways. He would, soon after the fight, marry Belinda Boyd, a devout Muslim, who immediately took the Muslim name of Kalilah Tolona. They would eventually start a family— three girls and a boy—Maryum, Jamillah, Muhammad, Jr., and Reesheda Ali.

In the meantime, Chris Dundee asked Cassius to go with him to the promoter's office. When they arrived, Clay told Rudy to stay outside. The whole scenario was strange, mysterious. Bill McDonald told Cassius he had to rid himself of his Black Muslim association, fire the cook, and security people, and publicly deny that he had joined the Nation of Islam.

Meanwhile, Cassius continued to refuse to lie about his religious convictions, and McDonald attempted to cancel the rematch with Liston.

As word got around about his association

with the Black Muslims, death threats piled up. People were afraid of the militant values the Black Muslims held and made more threats. Ali became paranoid. He said openly that he didn't trust anyone around him—not even his three closest supporters: Angelo Dundee, Doctor Pacheco, or Bundini Brown. He found it difficult to concentrate or sleep.

Amidst rumors of cancellation, the fight did go on.

When the gates opened for the fight, the police searched women's pocketbooks for concealed weapons. Some of the reporters covering the fight brought bullet-proof shields for the backs of their seats. Yet the distractions of the previous days vanished when Ali entered the ring.

The referee for the big event was to be Jersey Joe Walcott, a former world champion himself. While he gave the mandatory instructions to the contenders, Ali and Liston stared at one another. And when the fight started, Liston came over to press Ali, but almost without life. He was forced to follow Ali around the ring, trying to hit him with jabs and stopping when he stopped.

In the first round Liston came out firing shots at Ali. He hoped to finish a pressured Ali early in the bout. Ali held back and let

Liston tire out. Then, he let him have it. Ali opened a gash across Liston's left cheekbone, just underneath his eye. He fought Liston with great confidence, moving gracefully around the ring, delivering well-thought jabs to weaken his opponent.

This was a new strategy for Ali, who was known for his dancing and jabbing style. This time, he would hold the ropes and let Liston tire, as he deflected the jolts delivered with his hands, arms, and elbows.

In the fifth round, however, Ali was irritated by liniment to the eye, "accidentally" wiped across his face by Liston. It temporarily blinded him, and he returned to his corner. He asked that the gloves be changed. Dundee, fearing the fight might have to be refought, instructed Ali to return to the ring. Cassius closed the irritated eye and continued to pummel Liston.

As the eye cleared up, the beating Liston endured worsened, and it was obvious to all that Muhammad Ali would win.

Then Liston threw a slow jab, trying to cut the ring short. Ali stepped back, and as Liston's jab brushed the side of his face Ali saw his opening. That punch had left Liston wide open for the straight right Ali hit him with, flooring the now stunned Liston. He had never seen the blow. Ali did not go to a neutral corner as Jersey Joe begun the count.

When Walcott at last persuaded him to go to his corner, Nat Fleischer, publisher of Ring Magazine, called the referee to the ropes and told him Liston had been down more than the required ten seconds. Although Liston was now up and both men were beginning to throw punches again, Walcott ordered the fight stopped.

Ali had beaten Liston the second time, by a technical knockout, in the first two minutes of the first round. There were immediate cries that the fight had been rigged (especially since the blow that knocked Liston down, simply took him off balance, he was immediately able to get up), but Jose' Torres, who had recently won the light heavyweight title, was at ringside, reporting the match for a Spanish radio station. He played back his tape and heard himself say, ". . . a perfect shot to the jaw, right on the button and Liston is down. He's badly hurt. He might not get up."

Most of the reporters and fight fans did not want to believe that Ali had beaten Liston, but Torres thought that Liston beat himself yet again through his fear, as held by many Americans, of the Black Muslims. Perhaps Torres was right.

Regardless, Ali was now the undisputed Heavyweight Champion of the World.

Ali's next defense was against Floyd Patterson, who had been the youngest heavyweight champion to that point in history when he had won the title on November 30, 1956. Three years later, Patterson was defeated by Ingemar Johannson; but nine months after that, he won the title back from Johannson, the first heavyweight in the history of the sport to do that.

Liston won his title from Patterson, knocking him down twice in the first round. Now Patterson insulted Ali at every opportunity. Once the contract was signed for the bout, Ali began the same antics he had become famous for since the first confrontation with Liston, and would continue to do throughout his career. He began calling Patterson "the rabbit," and one time brought a package of carrots to Patterson's training quarters.

Ali announced that for the first time he would deliberately give his opponent a beating and would drag the fight out with Patterson far longer than would be necessary. Jose' Torres watched the fight on closed circuit TV, and reported that in the first round Ali failed to throw a single punch. He danced around, pulling back and inviting Patterson to make the

Shown here with the Mayor of Los Angeles, Tom Bradley, Muhammad Ali engages some light conversation about the up-coming L.A.'s Tribute to Muhammad Ali—and perhaps the Mayor's running for California governor.

first moves.

In the third round, it was evident that Patterson's back began to impair him. After that, he concentrated on defending himself rather than being on the attack. Many people thought Ali was tormenting him, taking advantage of the situation. They jeered and called out for the referee to stop the bout, but Torres thought Ali was unable to land the needed knockout blow. Finally, he stopped the bout in the twelfth round.

A few months later, in February of 1966, while training for his third title defense against Ernie Terrell, the word came that the Louisville draft board had reviewed his status and changed it from 1-Y, deferred status, that is, someone physically or otherwise impaired to be drafted, to 1-A, fully eligible for immediate induction into the Armed Forces. Ali had twice flunked the written examination for the draft as well, scoring 16 points when the passing grade was 17. But for him, the rules were changed and the passing grade was lowered to 15. He was offered several opportunities to take a commission in the special services branch of any of the Armed Services, which would mean that he would never see live fire or carry a weapon for that matter. But his religious convictions were just too strong, he refused. It didn't matter that he wouldn't be directly responsible for the death of the enemy, his religion dictated a total avoidance of military affiliation to the United States. When reporters came to ask Ali what he thought of the decision, he replied simply, "I ain't got no quarrel with the Viet Cong."

This would be a remembered statement.

If there had been outrage and criticism before, now it had increased ten-fold, perhaps a hundred-fold. The phones in his working office began to ring off the hook day in and out. The calls came from all over the world, commenting on his statement and his apparent lack of patriotism in defending the political position of the United States of America. One call, however, came from England—from Bertrand Russell. Muhammad Ali had never heard of the famous English philosopher before, but was pleased to find Russell agreeing with his stance on the war in Vietnam. He invited the famed philosopher to the return bout with Henry Cooper, which was held in London.

Bertrand Russell was unable to make the engagement, but for the next few years they regularly corresponded through cards and notes. It was two years later before Ali realized just who this famous correspondent was, when he saw a picture of Russell in an encyclopedia. Although they failed to meet at the Cooper fight as planned, Ali discovering his naivete', planned another trip to Great Britain, just to meet Russell. He tried desperately to renew his long suspended passport, but the State Department was unbending. Russell, old and in frail health, died before Ali could make the trip.

The Ernie Terrell fight was scheduled to be held in Chicago, but when Ali had stated publicly that he would not be drafted, Mayor Richard Daley, perhaps the most powerful politician at the time, told Governor Kerner of Illinois to direct the state athletic commission review, and of course deny his permit to fight.

Many of Ali's supporters wanted him to appear before the commission and say that he had been misquoted. Ben Bentley, Chicago promoter of the Ali-Terrell fight, flew to Miami for a clandestine meeting with Ali. If the fight was canceled, Bentley would be wiped out, financially. He asked Ali to call the commissioner and say he would make a public apology before the commission.

But when Ali appeared before the Athletic Commission of Illinois, his only apology was that he should have made his statements to the draft board, and not just to hounding reporters.

The fight was banned in Illinois; then in Louisville, Bangor, Maine, and Huron, South Dakota. Finally, the promoters moved north of the border, announcing the fight would be held in Montreal. But the controversy led to an immediate cancellation of the bout. Then it moved to a Montreal suburb, Verdun, next to Edmonton, Alberta, and then to a river town in Quebec—Sorel. Each time the local sponsors backed out eventually. At last, the fight was moved to Toronto.

A substitute opponent was provided in Canadian Heavyweight Champion George Chuvalo. The Province of Ontario was a member of the WBA, and so while the fight advertised as a "heavyweight showdown" with Ali representing the people of the United States and Chuvalo representing Canada, it wasn't a sanctioned fight.

Pressure groups closed and boycotted the closed circuit TV outlets until the gate shrank from an originally estimated three million dollars to a small fraction of that sum. Only 7500 paid to see the closed circuit broadcast, which grossed only $125,000.

Chuvalo was a body puncher with a granite chin; he had never been stopped in his forty-eight fights, and he absorbed all of the punish-

Shown here with Veronica Porshe, Ali leaves a crowded theater. It was said that Ms. Porshe was simply a companion

*to the champ, but after his divorce from Belinda Boyd in 1975,
the two were quickly married.*

ment Ali could give him. The Canadian consistently hit Ali below the belt but never drew a warning or a penalty from the referee. Yet even the referee gave Chuvalo only two of the fifteen rounds, while the other two judges gave him only one.

Facing almost immediate induction into the Army, Ali now began a tour of Europe that matched him for a second time with Henry Cooper in London, and then with Brian London in the city of the same name. The Cooper-Ali fight was not for a title, but the London fight was. He stopped Cooper in the sixth round and Brian London in the third.

A month later, Ali had one of the toughest fights in his career when he faced Karl Mildenberger in Frankfurt, Germany. Mildenberger was a lefty and as always, southpaws gave Ali trouble. But he managed to knock out the German in the twelfth round, which meant that he had eliminated every European contender he was matched against.

Ali returned to the States, and met Cleveland Williams in the Houston Astrodome. Williams had given Sonny Liston trouble when they met, but Ali was unbeatable. Williams dropped in three rounds.

And now the Ali-Terrell match was on again. Terrell's managers decided that their fighter's style was unorthodox enough to give Ali trouble, after viewing the Mildengerger-Ali bout; and Terrell was a stronger fighter than the German. Three months after the Cleveland Williams match, the two world champions faced off in the Astrodome before 37,321 paying customers.

It was not a good fight, in the sense it wasn't entertaining. Terrell was a sloppy fighter who missed with his first jab, and continued to miss throughout the confrontation. Ali was by far the better man, and there was no doubt early on as to the final outcome, even though the fight went the full fifteen rounds.

Six weeks later, Ali met Zora Folley at Madison Square Garden in his last bout before forced induction into the United States Army. Folley had a record of seventy-one victories, seven defeats and four draws in the ten years he had been ranked as a contender.

Jose' Torres saw the fight, and reported that Folley was the first experienced fighter he had ever seen terrified before his match. By the sixth round, the paying customers began to walk out. Ali ended it in the following round.

Chapter Seven

Uncle Sam
Takes His Toll

AS CASSIUS CLAY, MUHAMMAD ALI HAD REQUESTED A transfer from the jurisdiction of the Louisville draft board to Houston. He wasn't naive about it, however. He knew that the best he could hope for was to delay the inevitable—a long court battle or possible imprisonment for draft evasion. After his transfer was completed, orders quickly came for his induction into the United States Armed Forces on April 28, 1967.

The U.S. Customs House in Houston was surrounded by crowds of fans, protesters, and reporters—mostly college students with ban-

Waylon Jennings was only one of the many performers who appeared in the 1982, L.A.'s Tribute to Muhammad Ali. Academy Award winning actor Louis Gosett, Jr. emceed the event.

ners reading "Stay Home, Muhammad Ali!"

The potential for rioting was so great that it was necessary for a U.S. Navy officer to usher him into a room with thirty other draftees for a written test, which was followed by the usual physical examination. When those were finished, the draftees were sent to another room for induction, where an officer called out the assignments. But when he called, "Cassius Clay—Army," Muhammad Ali did not step forward with the others.

When it became clear that the man still known to the United States Government as Cassius Clay wasn't going to allow himself to be drafted; Ali was charged and tried for draft evasion.

The judge who heard the case handed down the maximum penalty for draft evasion, better known as "draft dodging," a sentence of five years in prison and a $10,000 fine. Ali appealed, of course, to the U.S. Court of Appeals. He hoped to have a better chance of winning by moving the case to the predominately black U.S. Court of Appeals in New Orleans, Louisiana. But it was not to be. There was far too much public outcry to punish him for his seemingly unpatriotic behavior, and the former decision was upheld.

Having lost his gamble with the United

States Justice System, the case now four years old, Lady Luck looked his way. The case was shortly thereafter chosen to be heard in the halls of the Supreme Court of the United States. Although it wouldn't be until 1971, more than three years in court, that he'd be exonerated, the fact that the High Court was deliberating the case gave Ali some leeway to be a WBA boxing contender.

But the WBA didn't wait for the government to make its final act; the boxing authority stripped Ali of his title in the meantime, announcing they would hold an elimination tournament to replace him as Champion, while New York State revoked his boxing license on a clerical technicality.

The first uneventful (elimination) fight was to be between Jimmy Ellis, a childhood friend of Ali's and undefeated champion in his own right, and a former meat-packer from Philadelphia Pennsylvania, Joe Frazier.

On February 16, 1970, Joe Frazier was made the official WBA Heavyweight Champion of the World.

During the years of his exile, Muhammad Ali earned his living by making appearances on college campuses all across the country, speaking out against the "police action" in Vietnam.

This candid shot was taken as Ali leaves a star-studded charity event in Los Angeles. With him (from left to right) are: Linda

Olsen, past associate editor of Holloway House/Melrose Square, model Bernard Gore, and James Anderson.

He was still barred from leaving the country, his passport still invalid. In Europe, he could have continued to fight, but the American government was determined to crush him into submission for his refusal to do what they said was the right and moral thing for him to do. Elvis Presley went to Germany, why should Ali not be drafted?

The contract with the Louisville sponsoring group had ended the previous year of Ali's scheduled induction into the Army, 1966. So, after the match with Karl Mildenberger in Frankfurt, Germany, Ali no longer had the lucrative sponsorship he'd had for six years.

The Champ needed to pull for support.

For several years, Ali's closest confidant and adviser had been Herbert Muhammad, one of the sons of the leader of the Nation of Islam, Elijah Muhammad. Ali had been through so much, he completely turned to his religion for solitude. It got to the point that he would allow only members of his faith to prepare his meals for fear of being poisoned.

Ali turned to the media for support as well. Although he had still managed to accumulate over $100,000.00 in a retirement fund, bills to Sonji, and attorneys' fees still haunted him.

A series of shows for TV were produced to show "What if. . ." Ali had fought Rocky Marciano, and who'd win. Elaborate computers were used to calculate the victories and Maricano, at 44, even made a TV appearance. The Champ made only $999.00 from the whole thing.

Johnny Carson, the famous nighttime talk show host who openly opposed the Government's treatment of Ali, brought him on the Tonight Show on several occasions to subdue the bad publicity that had mounted against the Champ.

By now, Herbert Muhammad took over as Ali's manager.

During Ali's twenty-six fights under the Louisville Millionaire Club, his gross earnings had been $2,376,115. Gordon Davidson, attorney for the Louisville group, said that the original fifty-fifty split was changed to sixty-forty, in Ali's favor, to help him through this bad period.

Yet, even the major portion of his share of this money was continuously being eaten up by the heavy legal expenses and by his newly-acquired standard of living. Although the break with his first wife was relatively amicable, he still owed Sonji over $150,000 in back alimony, $250,000 in legal fees, and many other debts as well. It would be a long time before he would be able to settle his accounts.

In his last three fights before exile, under Herbert Muhammad, Ali earned $1,265,000—not a bad living but just half of what he was used to earning—and now he was at his prime.

There were many attempts during the years of exile to promote fights for Ali, but the answer was always the same—no. Thirty-eight different states turned down his applications for re-instatement to the WBA. The American Legion was most persistent of all Ali-opposers, and under this pressure the local athletic commissions always gave in.

But just as things seemed most dark, Ali received a phone call from Georgia State Senator Leroy Johnson, the most powerful black politician in the state. Johnson knew what pressure to bring to win Ali a license not from the state government, but from the City of Atlanta. Blacks controlled most political power in that metropolis, and the governor was sure of success.

The license came through, but now Joe Frazier, had become the official champion. For Ali to regain his title he'd have to fight Frazier.

Frazier's managers backed out, claiming they had a prior commitment for Joe Frazier to fight Bob Foster for the title. And so a substitute was made: Ali's first fight after his years in exile would be with Jerry Quarry.

Many of Ali's friends, and most of his enemies, felt that the years of laying off had drained him. He was older and not in the top condition he had been for past fights. Never before had a fighter come back after three years away from the ring to regain his title.

Also, the fight in Atlanta would be a test to the sovereignty of the people of the State of Georgia, being the only state to grant Ali a license. In order to do so, an exhibition bout was held first in the 2,000 seat Morehouse College Gym; more than 5,000 people showed up.

But the rumors of Ali's physical condition proved true—Ali quickly tired as he faced three sparring partners, but a heart-felt pep talk from Bundini Brown, and the faith of his associate trainers, soon restored his confidence in himself. When the exhibition ended, the crowd roared its approval.

He would be psychologically ready for Quarry. After the contract was signed, Ali flew down to Miami Beach to train, and then moved to Atlanta for the last two weeks before the Quarry fight. But just before his entourage left the hotel in Miami, two giftwrapped packages were delivered to his suite—what would be an attempt to break down his newly found confidence.

Muhammad Ali is warmly welcomed at the White House by then President Jimmy Carter for a dinner following the signing

of the new Panama Canal Treaty. Ali is shown here giving the President two tickets to his fight with Ernie Shavers.

Blue Lewis, Ali's sparring partner, read the message enclosed: "To Cassius Clay from Georgia." He then opened it to find the body of a little black chihuahua, decapitated. A message within the "gift" box read: "We know how to handle black draftdodging dogs in Georgia. Stay out of Atlanta!"

The other box held a rag doll in conspicuous yellow shorts and tiny boxing gloves. A rope was tied around its throat and the head was jerked to the side in imitation of a lynching.

When Ali reached Atlanta, Senator Johnson gave him the use of his own cottage on a man made lake. Angelo Dundee, his manager, wanted him to stay in the city, but Ali liked the cottage. There were bomb threats, as before, but he discounted and tried to ignore them.

Then early one morning when Ali made ready for his road work while it was still dark, he opened the door and stepped off the porch.

A gun shot sounded out, followed by a second.

Ali dropped to the ground as more shots rang out, and then crawled back to the cottage while three men taunted him from the darkness. More shots followed, and then Bundini produced two pistols (that he was not legally supposed to have) and returned the fire.

A few minutes later, the phone rang: it was the three, scared off by Bundini's shots. They informed Bundini that the incident was a warning for Ali not to enter the ring, the caller saying he was willing to die to keep the fight from taking place.

The fight was almost anticlimactic: Ali stopped Quarry in three rounds. But he was tired at the end, many of his punches were off target—Ali was still not at a hundred percent. There were openings he could not take, and openings he was lucky Quarry missed. The fight was won when Ali opened a deep gash over Quarry's eye, blood pouring out so profusely that the fight had to be stopped.

Despite the victory, though, it was understood that if it had gone the full ten rounds, those who predicted that Ali was finished might have been proven right.

The next match for Ali was against Oscar Bonavena, the Argentinian who a few years later was shot and killed while working as a security guard at the Mustang Ranch brothel near Reno, Nevada. Bonavena was a strongman with little wit, but extremely dangerous in the ring because of his shear strength. Jose' Torres, who had sparred with him once, said that unlike most boxers, who try to hit their opponent without being hit in return, Bonavena's philosophy was, "You hit me and I hit you. Let's see who falls first."

The bout was set for December 7, 1970—Pearl Harbor Day. The patriots—The American Legion in particular, protested loudly and did everything within their power to stop the fight, but without success. New York State had been forced to return Ali's license when it was shown that the State Athletic Commission had granted licenses to ninety fighters convicted of embezzlement, rape and murder.

The odds were six to one in Ali's favor, and in the opening rounds, it appeared that the old Ali had returned. But Bonavena did not surrender. The Argentinian returned time and time again, chasing Ali even when most of his punches missed their designated targets.

Ali predicted Bonavena would fall in nine, but the fight went the full fifteen rounds. It was almost an even match through the first fourteen; if Bonavena could have come back strongly in the last round, the match might have been his.

But Ali finally knocked Bonavena down. The Argentinian got up on the count of nine, and was floored again. Once more he struggled to his feet, to be dropped for the third time. The fight was over; three times down in one round, and Ali had scored a TKO.

With no excuse, legal or otherwise, Joe Frazier would have to meet Ali. The match was set for March 8, 1971.

They called the Ali-Frazier match the rarest event in sports history. For the first time two undefeated heavyweight champions were to meet in the ring for the largest purse of all time—five million dollars. The newspapers had printed the photostats of the two 2.5 million dollar checks. If the fight went the full fifteen rounds, that would work out to fifty-five thousand five-hundred fifty-five dollars and fifty-five cents for each fighter each minute. Almost nine-hundred and twenty-six dollars for each second. Incredible.

The fight at Madison Square Garden would be viewed by the largest closed circuit television audience in history. Promoter Jerry Perenchio was predicting a worldwide gross of forty million dollars. When Muhammad Ali heard the prediction he was tempted to ask Joe Frazier to demand an even larger share; but it was too late. There'd be no more talking until they met in the ring.

The money was incredible, but even more incredible was the fact that this match was happening at all. When Muhammad Ali refused induction into the United States Armed

Ali is seen here chatting with the then famed married acting duo, Leon and Jayne Kennedy. Leon went on to produce films,

while his wife became one of the first female sports broad-casters for a major network.

Forces, his title was taken away, his boxing license was revoked in virtually every state, his passport was lifted by the State Department. They said he was finished, washed up, through. They said he would never fight again in America or in any other country.

Joe Frazier won recognition by winning one minor title after another until the WBA had to let him contend for the championship. Then by beating Jimmy Ellis, who had been recognized as champion of the World Boxing Association at that time, although he'd been inactive for years.

Ellis was a boyhood friend of Ali's, and had often worked with him as a sparring partner. Frazier stopped Ellis in four rounds. And, because Ellis had been an Ali sparring partner, Frazier learned a little of what he'd be up against.

The day finally came, March 8, 1971. Although there had been preliminary bouts (one that included Ali's brother) much of the audience paid little attention. The main bout would follow, and everyone was anxious to see Muhammad Ali.

Then the moment came; the crowd went wild as Ali came down the aisle, wearing white trunks with red stripes and a short robe.

Joe Frazier was dressed much more

gaudily—velvet brocade robe, green and gold, announcer Johnny Addie introduced the fighters, and then referee Arthur Mercante moved into the ring. Ali turned away to offer a silent prayer to Allah, the Muslim god, and then the bell rang for round one.

The fighters met in the center of the ring, Ali circling around while Frazier walked straight towards him from the corner. Ali withdrew then threw a series of jabs, many of which missed. Frazier connected with the first blow of the fight, a right cross to Ali's chest. But when the bell rang, the round belonged to Ali, on the scores of those short jabs.

Ali had the advantage of a longer reach—82 inches as compared to Frazier's 73.5 inches. Frazier had to move in close to connect, but Ali could hit while standing outside the other's effective area of power. Frazier waited while Ali moved in, repeatedly jabbing. The round again belonged to Ali, but during the last twenty seconds Frazier began to apply pressure on his opponent.

The third round was no contest: Ali lost it when Frazier drove him to the ropes and kept him there. This was once a tactic Ali used to tire his opponent, but this time it was getting to him. The match now seemed in Frazier's favor. He won the fourth round, and again met

Ali in his corner when the bell rang to start the fifth. After the first three rounds, Ali stood during the one minute rest period; but after the fourth, he sat on his stool, bleary-eyed and noticeably diminished.

During the fifth round, Ali started to press Frazier, but too late to decisively win the round. Both fighters worked under tremendous pressure imposed on each other, by each other; both realized they were facing the toughest battle of their careers. Frazier maintained the same steady pace in the sixth round but Ali moved more. And at the end of the seventh round, Jose' Torres' scorecard showed four rounds for Ali, three for Frazier.

Both fighters were working hard, giving everything they had; but it was not the best fight they ever fought. The long lay-off was still having an affect on Ali's usual speed. In the eight round, the fighters took turns poking fun at each other, daring and taunting each other. Ali was spending much of his time taking blows at the ropes, a technique learned early in his career to tire his opponent.

The eighth round belonged to Frazier, given away by Ali. The match was even, now. But in the ninth, Ali came out like gangbusters, and had his best round since round two. Then in the tenth, Ali once more seemed to lose the reserve of strength he had previously drawn on, doing nothing until the last twenty seconds or so while Frazier chased around the ring him relentlessly.

In the eleventh, Frazier tagged Ali with a left hook to the button, and then bore in with a series of vicious blows until Ali's legs began to buckle. Ali's eyes became glassy, but somehow he managed to stay on his feet, something he was known to have the ability to do. Even Bonavena's roundhouse punches previously, could not bring him to his knees.

The twelfth round was also Fraziers'; if Ali was to win, he had to take the next three in a row. Yet, Frazier continued to bear down on Ali heavily, and again took another round. But it wasnt' over. Ali came alive during the fourteenth, showing something of the Ali of days thought long passed. The round was his. He still had a chance to win, however small.

Frazier ordered his body to move out and meet Ali, and landed a deadly left hook to Ali's jaw. Ali fell flat on his back. As the referee began the count, Ali tried to focus his eyes, and came to his feet on the count of three. The fight was not over until the bell rang, but there was no doubt of who the winner would be.

A unanimous decision for Frazier.

Ali gave his all that night. What more could he give?

Ali had lost. But the career he had attained to this point was astounding. Muhammad Ali won his first twenty-nine professional fights in a row, twenty-three by a knockout. Adding in his amateur record of 161 wins in 167 matches, Muhammad Ali is the most phenomenally successful boxer in the history of the sport, the man who brought boxing back to worldwide popularity at a time when it seemed in danger of dying. Professional fighters couldn't beat him. People who hated him for his religion and for his race couldn't stop him. Only the power of the United States Government had managed to stop him—for awhile.

Muhammad Ali shown, clowns with replica of King Kong to introduce the Dino De Laurentis release of The Big Party, *a salute to new sports and the performing arts.*

Chapter Eight

The Greatest Comeback of All Time

B Y THE TIME MUHAMMAD ALI fought his thirty-second bout, The Greatest had tasted the bitterness of defeat. Joe Frazier became the undisputed champion of the world. The crown was gone, for Ali, lost as only a champion could lose—in the arena of competition.

Some thought that Ali would give up, quit. For in his bitter sweet predictions for himself, he had hinted that a loss would force a retirement. And, there were critics who were furious at the idea of him continuing his career even after he'd lost his title.

The voice and animated likeness of Heavyweight champ Muhammad Ali, played a modern-day Robin Hood in NBC's Saturday childrens' show I Am the Greatest.

This opposition only made him more determined to make a comeback, to revive the spirit of the sport he so truly loved. But, lose or win, Ali would always be known as the greatest boxer of our time.

On June 28, 1971, nearly four months after his loss to Frazier, Ali won a different battle—one that had plagued him for years—the Supreme Court of the United States overturned his conviction on charges of draft evasion.

With this off his mind, Ali was free to travel the States, again touring college campuses, speaking about human rights and himself, his religious convictions, and the legal battle, which finally ended in victory. And there was another agenda—now he was training for a match against an ex-sparring mate, Jimmy Ellis.

The fight would be held in the Houston Astrodome on July 26, 1971. Although Ali had a lot of his personal popularity, fans still crowded the arena to see him defeated. This fight was anticlimactic—his old friend was slower and less talented. The fight was won in the twelfth round by a knockout.

Technically, the win wasn't anything to brag about. But psychologically, it worked for Ali, who now wanted to prepare for his next bout. Despite his returning enthusiasm for boxing, it would be three years before the rematch—between he and Frazier—would happen. And, by that time Frazier would be defeated by the young George Foreman a one-time Olympic champion in his own right.

Still, his motivation for the rematch would gain momentum in the successive years, and Ali trained as hard as ever. Matches were set up to prepare him for the second Frazier bout. It didn't matter to Ali that Frazier had been beaten. The fact that Frazier had beaten him plagued him and he wanted to reclaim that victory. He began training.

In November of that year, Ali would win a decisive victory over Buster Mathis, at the Houston Astrodome, where Ali was now making his home. He then began a world-wide tour, which would take him to Zurich to meet Jurgen Blin. Again, the match was no contest, Ali would knock his opponent out in seven.

To the Orient. In Tokyo, Japan he met Mac Foster and easily beat him. However, because Foster had staying power, the fight went to fifteen. The following month he met George Chuvalo in Vancouver, British Columbia—for the second time—and then he moved on for Jerry Quarry in June of the following year.

Similarly, this was the second time that Ali met Quarry in the ring. But this time, Quarry

Muhammad Ali and Veronica Porsche greet guests at the preview of Mohammad, Messenger Of God. *Here Ali is shown*

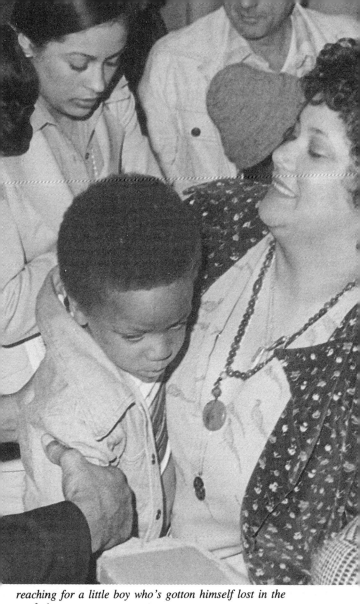

reaching for a little boy who's gotton himself lost in the confusion.

was in better shape, despite the passing of years, and Ali found it more difficult to stop him. It went seven, being stopped in that round by the referee because Quarry had been noticeably hurt, buckling and dazed.

Interestingly, it was Ali, not Quarry who asked for the fight to be stopped. The ref was slow to react, and Ali, in adherence of his religious ideals, didn't want to really hurt Quarry. Late in the round the fight was ended.

This win would ignite, a new found fire in Ali. He felt like the Phoenix, rising from his own ashes. Another exhibition fight was set up for Ali in Dublin, Ireland. This time it would be another of his sparring partners, a man named Al "Blue" Lewis. In the boxing circuit, Lewis was known as one of the hardest hitters—and Ali knew it.

Muhammad knew, though, that if he were to really make a come back, he'd have to test the limits of his endurance. Having been a workout partner of Ali's, Lewis knew that his friend had an Achilles Heal—the rib cage. Sure enough, Lewis managed to bruise Ali's ribs, an injury that dated back to his fight with Jimmy Ellis before he won the title from Sonny Liston in 1970.

But this injury meant more to Ali. At the word that Ali's ribs had been hurt again, another trauma would have postponed, perhaps ended his return to the ring.

Ali went ahead and met Quarry, and won in three rounds, too soon to hurt the now-healing ribs. This was a relatively easy match, as opposed to the Lewis fight, which went to eleven.

Now, he would meet with Floyd Patterson again having to prove himself after seven years when Ali had beaten him badly the first time. Patterson gave it a good effort, but lost in the seventh round. The string of success for Ali was set. Bob Foster would be the next victory, dropping in the eighth round in a fight held in Lake Tahoe, Nevada.

But Ali would stay in Nevada—Las Vegas, Glitter Gulch—to meet Joe Bugner for the first of two matches. While in Vegas, Ali met up with the King Of Rock 'n Roll, Elvis Presley, who gave Ali a glittering robe with the words, THE PEOPLE'S CHAMPION, embossed on the back.

It was evident to boxing experts that Bugner was a stronger man than Ali had met in any of his recent matches. Still, Ali won by a decision in the twelfth. Next it was to San Diego where he would meet Ken Norton, an unknown fighter at that time. But this fight would prove fame for Norton, and defeat for Ali.

Ken Norton was a hometown boy from San Diego—and a young man. Ali was now over thirty, thirty-two as a matter of fact, considered old for a fighter. And, Ali was tired out from his series of previous engagements, while he had also begun ignoring his once rigorous rules of training. He had become comfortable, and thought that Norton would be just another push-over for him.

However, in the second round of the bout, Norton landed a crushing blow to Ali's jaw. Dundee and Bundini Brown rushed in to stop the fight, but Ali refused. Joe Frazier and Archie Moore were there to witness the event and hopefully Ali's downfall—and to coach the inexperienced Norton. Ali felt backed into the proverbial "corner" and wanted to send the lot home, disappointed.

Now it was discovered that the jaw was broken. And, even with a broken jaw, the decision was a split. One judge had calculated Ali as the victor.

Because of Ali's setback in the loss to Norton it was inevitable that a second match would have to be fought. But instead there was a twist of fate: Dick Sadler, Foreman's manager, was impressed with Ali's performance and paid him a visit. Sadler asked Ali to hold out after his jaw had healed to fight

Foreman rather than to fight Norton a second time. This would mean a lot of money for the two fighters—for Ali could always draw a crowd.

Ali asked Sadler to let him think about it. But in his mind all he could think about was Norton, Norton, Norton—he just had to have the man who barely beat him. He called Dick on the phone and turned his offer down flat.

The rematch against Norton would take Ali back to the West Coast—to Hollywood, to Los Angeles, California. The publicity was like only Hollywood could create, and the fight was brutal. Ali came out ahead this time, winning in the twelfth round. Almost two months later he fought Rudi Lubbers, a hulking Dutchman, in Djakarta, the capital of Indonesia. Again, the decision was in Ali's favor. But like his namesake Muhammad who took it to the mountain, Ali wasn't through—nearly three years after he lost his title to Joe Frazier, a rematch was set for January 28, 1974.

The bout was hard fought and Frazier wasn't going to lie down. But after twelve of the most hard hitting rounds in the history of the sport, Frazier went down. Again, Muhammad Ali was the Greatest.

Beating Frazier wiped out the idea of losing from Ali's mind. And, it also meant a

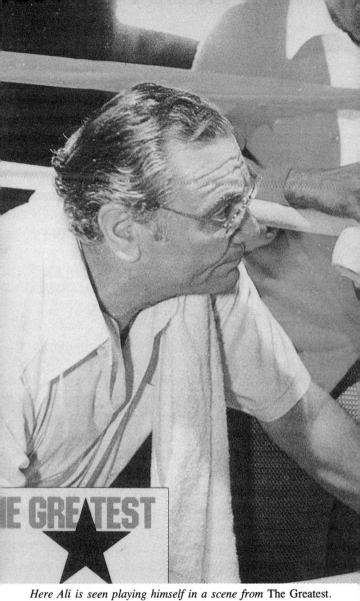

Here Ali is seen playing himself in a scene from The Greatest. *His white trainer and companion, Joe Martin, was played by*

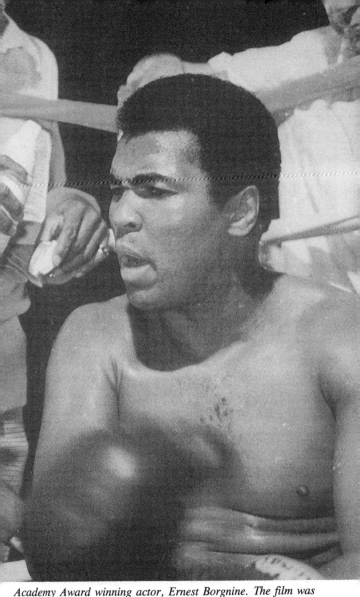

Academy Award winning actor, Ernest Borgnine. The film was very well received by the public.

From The Greatest *a reinactment of the famouse first round knockout of Sonny Liston in the second Ali-Liston match. This*

knockout is one of the most remembered in boxing history, and causes disagreements among boxing fans to this day.

multi-million dollar win for Ali, who's finances had dwindled after his eight-year suspension from the National Boxing Association. From here on out, there would be no purses smaller than one-million dollars, and Ali would be known as one of the greatest money earners in sports history.

Now it was to the homeland, Africa. Ali had been there before where he had become a Continental hero. Zaire was the first Third-World nation to sponsor an international sporting event, though, others would be held in Manila, and Kuala Lumpur, Malaysia. All would have one thing in common—Muhammad Ali.

Ali would meet George Foreman in Zaire and was guaranteed a purse of over five-million. Foreman knew he was training for the fight of his life. Like Ali, Foreman concentrated on diet and roadwork. But Foreman was even more diligent—he ran mountain trails uphill. The possibility of fifteen rounds crossed George Foreman's mind, a thing he had never faced before.

The match was set for October 30, 1974.

When the two fighters finally reached the training ring in Kinshasa, Zaire, they sparred in the same modern gym in the capital, Ali took no hesitation at examining his opponent. George seemed fleshy to Ali, but he was building his stamina by timing his rounds at four minutes with thirty second rest periods between.

Foreman trained hard; he became a driven man. He thought that Ali had tarnished his championship title by being, "The People's Champion," and he was jealous at the thought.

About a week before the scheduled match, Foreman received a sharp blow from a sparring partner, which cut his eye. Rumors spread that the fight would be canceled. Ali became paranoid, a state he admits to and is not proud of, and sent a messenger to President Mobuto so that Foreman would not be allowed to leave the country. No one knows for sure if the President issued the order, but Foreman remained in Zaire, having canceled vacation plans to recover, and to possibly see a doctor for his injury, in Paris, France.

The fight was set at the un-Godly hour of four in the morning so as to have a prime-time fight of nine in the evening, New York time. It was held in a converted African arena that had been originally built by colonial Belgians.

Odds around the betting world favored Foreman: 4-1 in the States, 2-1 in London, and 3-1 in the European Common. The thought that Ali was too old was of great concern, and although he had many moral supporters, bookies gave the fight to Foreman.

Back in Zaire, Ali entered the ring. He did his usual routine of talking to the crowd, which only strengthened his psychological picture. Foreman stalled his entrance for over ten minutes, which might have cost him the fight.

Zack Clayton refereed the match, and while he gave the two the usual instructions for the fight, Ali taunted Foreman who withdrew at the jeering. Even though Clayton warned Ali to literally ". . . shut your mouth. . ." Ali continued, pointing out that there was no rules about talking.

At the bell, Ali came out dancing. Foreman was aggressive and was able to get to Muhammad Ali. Foreman cut Ali off, and Ali became noticeably irritated at his adversary's moves. He was forced to change his strategy, and go to the ropes.

George Foreman was a strong, formidable man. Ali knew this, having listened to Bossman.

In the second round of the fight, Foreman landed a right to Ali's skull, nearly knocking him senseless. Then shots to Ali's midsection were made, to the kidneys, fulfilling the reputation that Foreman had created for himself. In boxing circles it was known that Foreman could give a good "legal" kidney punch. Ali took to the ropes again, and he began to taunt Foreman with insults that he hoped would give the time to fully regain his stamina.

Foreman had made a prediction of his own: "Ali the Flea, will fall in three. . ." But Ali was relentless in his tongue-lashing of Foreman. The referee continued to warn him to be quiet, but the former champ refused.

Just after another verbal assault from Ali, Foreman came out landing thrusts that stunned Ali. Foreman began to move in for the kill, but Ali managed to stall until the bell rang.

In the following round, Foreman, confident of his advantage, stood straight up, jabbing, leaving himself open for Ali. Ali came out, and pummeled Foreman with a series of lefts that left the champion in a daze.

This was only the third time in his career that Foreman had to go longer than eight rounds, and the pace was taking a toll on him. But it was doubly hard on the now-struggling Ali.

In that eighth round, Foreman, determined to punish and embarrass Ali, threw his most powerful punch. Ali ducked and recoiled out of harm's way. Foreman went to the ropes and Ali began to pound the younger man. Foreman turned to face Ali, but only met with a right cross to his chin.

Now Foreman was still dazed from the punishment Ali had inflicted on him. His eyes became glazed, something was amiss— Foreman began to lean, and finally fell. It was over, Muhammad Ali was again Heavyweight Champion of the World.

The match went eight exciting rounds— many of which were very closely scored. But Ali was the victor by a TKO.

After winning the bout, known as "The Rumble In The Jungle," Ali took home a purse of $5,450,000.

In Kuala Lumpur, Ali met Joe Bugner for the second time. This time he would take home less, but it was still over two-million for the victory. Next he would meet Joe Frazier for the third time in Manila—winning the highest purse yet—six-million dollars!

This match was set for October 1, 1975 and would be known in boxing history as "The Thriller In Manila." A slight scandal emerged as Ali prepared for the bout. Accompanying him to Manila was the beautiful Veronica Porche, who'd eventually become Ali's third wife.

Yet, there was another scandal for Ali to overcome. It was discovered that just prior to this series of fights between 1974 and 1975, which led to Ali's reclaiming of the championship title, he had hired a man named Bossman Jones, who had spent over a month sparring with his opponent, Foreman—possibly giving Ali an advantage.

It was a slight embarrassment, but Ali let none of it bother him, made no comments, and continued his training program, throughout.

Regardless, he was now the King, The Greatest, The Heavyweight Champion of the World.

A candid photo from L.A.'s Salute to Muhammad Ali. Here the Champ is shown flanked by Louis Gossett, Jr., who emceed the

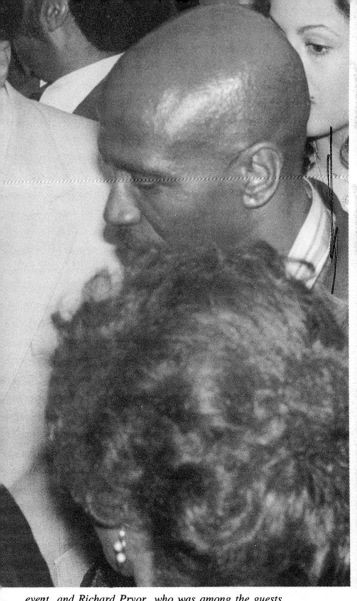

event, and Richard Pryor, who was among the guests.

Chapter Nine

In The Aftermath

$\mathbf{A}$FTER THE FOREMAN FIGHT, retirement rose on the horizon for Muhammad Ali—or many so thought. Conversation about the inevitable came up again and again over for the next few years. Several times Ali called news conferences announcing his retirement—only to change his mind afterward. Nobody knew if he was serious or just pulling one of his publicity stunts.

And, he had other problems to take care of. Belinda, Ali's second wife, although a Muslim herself, found the continuing strictness of the customs of Islam too much for her to deal with

Pen in hand, Ali gets ready to sign another autograph. The book signing was sponsored by Disneyland July 2, 1991, for his authorized biography, Muhammad Ali *by Thomas Hauser.*

and, filed for a divorce. She was also aware of her husband's traveling companion, Veronica Porche. It was January, 1977.

On April 18, 1977, Belinda was granted custody of their four children, receiving two-million dollars as a cash settlement along with an apartment in Chicago, a house in the suburbs of that same city, and two cars.

But Ali was not to stay single for long. In June of that same year, he married for the third time to Veronica Porche, rumored to be his "companion" for some years by that time.

By 1977 world awareness about the drought in Africa had increased. And Muhammad Ali, answered the call, by announcing that fifty cents of each closed-circuit subscription of his up-coming fight with Chuck Wepner would be donated to the effort. It is estimated that after the fight was held in Cleveland, Ohio the donation had reached a whopping three-hundred thousand dollars. This money was split equally between Africare, a private organization, and the United Nations' Children's Relief Fund.

By 1977, Ali slowed down, fighting only two matches that year against Alfredo Evagelista and Earnie Shavers—winning both in fifteen rounds. The Champ was slowing down. He continued traveling the world, meeting heads of state everywhere he went. He began to be known for humanitarian reasons and received numerous honors.

At this time, Leon Spinks was a rising star in the boxing world. And, in 1978, Ali would fall to the fiery youth.

The match was staged at the Las Vegas Hilton, February 15, 1978. Leon Spinks, ten years Ali's junior at 26, while admired as a good boxer was considered by some as a "bum of the month." He had gained his boxing reputation boxing in the Marine Corps and had only won seven professional bouts.

Spinks' style was wild and untrained— something that left Ali off balance. Spinks came out flailing punches and cornering the Champ many times. Ali tried to out maneuver the younger fighter, but Spinks' unpredictability proved to work in his favor.

The fight went the full fifteen rounds. The crowd, it was clear, thought Ali had won. Surprisingly, though, when the scorecards were tallied, Spinks was the victor, by a split decision.

Like the feelings expressed with the first Norton loss, Ali was determined to have a rematch. If he were to retire, he wanted to retire as the undisputed Champ.

A rematch with Spinks was arranged, this

time it would be held in the Superdome in New Orleans, Louisiana on September 15, 1978.

Unlike the small crowd that witnessed the first bout between the two, 70,000 fans paid an estimated six-million dollars, while ABC televised the match, beaming it to an audience of two billion in over eighty countries!

Spinks, overconfident, spent the week prior to the bout in the seedy bars of the French Quarter of New Orleans. Although he was found and attempts to sober him up were made, it is said that he spent the night before the fight carousing with some of "the boys."

Ali came out as a professional. Although he outweighed Spinks by twenty pounds, he gracefully jabbed at the younger man, while Spinks tried to keep balance. By the fifth round, Ali was pummeling Spinks with combinations that drew boxing fans back to an earlier time. The second fight, like the first, went the full fifteen.

When the match was over, there was a buzzing of unsureness in the crowd. But Ali, realizing his impending victory, still the showman yelled "I danced, I danced fifteen with the twenty-five year old boy."

Spinks said about the fight: "He was always my idol—he still is."

The fight was also lucrative. Muhammad Ali

received over three-million for the event.

Of the three judges, one scored eleven rounds, Ali, the other two, ten—at the age of thirty-six, Muhammad Ali became the Heavyweight Champion of the World for an unprecedented third time.

Commenting on his victory Ali said, "God, I have suffered and suffered. It really hurts. It's time for a new life now. I don't want to fight no more. I've been doing it for twenty-five years and you can only do so much wear to the body. It changes a man. It has changed me. I can see it. I can feel it."

This began a retirement of two years, years spent with Veronica and their two children.

But the constant need for money was a thorn in the side of the champion. Although he'd earned over fifty million dollars by the second Spinks fight, the financial weight he carried on his shoulders was too great.

Then in 1980, at the age of thirty-eight, he would meet Larry Holmes in the ring, a sparring partner, whom he had brought to Africa for the Foreman fight.

In the meantime, Ali had been prescribed a drug, Thyrolar, which controlled a worsening thyroid condition.

The fight was scheduled for October 2, 1980 to be held at the Hilton Hotel in Las Vegas.

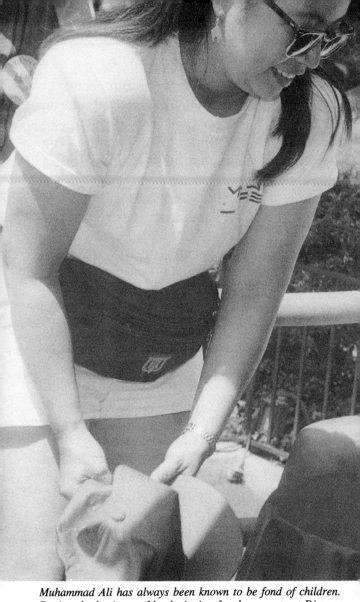

Muhammad Ali has always been known to be fond of children. During the business of book signing for the parents at Disney-

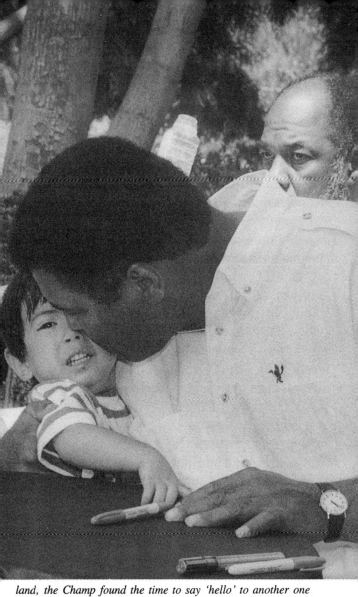

land, the Champ found the time to say 'hello' to another one of his littlest fans.

And although the fight lasted eleven rounds, Holmes defeated Ali. The two were friends and confidants said that Holmes was as gentle as possible with Ali. But after suffering a cut under his right eye, and a bloody nose that wouldn't quit, Ali was advised by Herbert Muhammad to throw in the towel—the fight was over.

Ali made a public statement that he had been sluggish during the Holmes fight because of the Thyrolar he had been only recently prescribed. He also blamed the drug for his bleeding nose.

By 1981, Ali had gotten his financial life in order and now wanted to make another comeback—only to learn that no one wanted to face him in the ring. And because of rumors of Parkinson's Disease looming about the superstar, it was unlikely that he'd be granted a license. Eventually he managed to get a permit to fight in the Bahamas. On December 11, 1981, he fought and lost a ten-round bout against Trevor Berbick.

This would be his last fight. By 1984, symptoms from the Parkinson's Disease and a condition that many fighters get—dementia pulgilistica—removed him from the ring permanently. The second diagnosis of dementia, caused by blows to the head was made by a prominent British doctor who went as far to say that Ali had received brain damage from blows to the head, although he'd never personally examined Ali.

Boxing fans knew differently.

Ali was slower these days, that was true, but until his last few fights Ali took very few blows to the head, having perfected the deflection technique with his arms and elbows. What has really slowed him up, physically, not mentally, is his athletic lifestyle and, of course age itself.

At this time, many organizations would begin to recognize him for his humanitarian efforts.

In 1982 Tom Bradley, Mayor of Los Angeles declared a "Muhammad Ali Day" and many stars were there: Lola Falana, Lou Rawls, Richard Pryor, Kenny Rogers, Waylon Jennings, Chevy Chase, Billy Crystal, Melissa Manchesher, and others. Academy Award winner, Louis Gosset, Jr., who emceed, said about Ali: "When I was growing up in Brooklyn, before Muhammad Ali, we were expected to speak soflty and know our place. But Ali changed all that...and instilled pride in us. That pride, black pride, Muhammad Ali instilled in me made me a stronger person—which enabled me to use that pride in my professional career."

But again, Ali would have a failed marriage. Later this same year, 1984, Veronica Porche was granted a divorce and custody of their two children.

And Ali did realize that his time in the ring was over, but that this fact would not be the end of his life and on November 19, 1986 he married Yolonda Williams.

By 1987, he involved himself in many real-estate developments both for average income and poor homes in the United States. He has a shoe-polish company, and even a perfume business. He has many business investments in the Middle East—especially Saudi Arabia.

He also continued his campaign to promote world peace. Today, he travels the United states with his new wife, Yolonda "Lonnie" Williams Ali, speaking about his trips to the Middle East, especially about his recent meeting with Sadam Hussein. He's a man's man, and philanthropist. A lover of children and children's causes, his foundation has donated thousands to children's organizations both in the United States and Africa.

His religion has also taken a prominent role in his life. He is still known as having a great sense of humor, and tries to take life as it comes. An example of this change from boxing champion to great humanitarian comes from Joe Nazel, journalist and writer.

He recalls a recent meeting with the champ in an impromptu gathering in Ali's hotel suite says Nazel: "Because of his religious beliefs he cannot knowingly dupe another human being. So, here is this guy, showing us card tricks in his room—laughing—and then showing us how to do them. He is really a great man."

And the only three-time Heavyweight Champion of the World.

RING RECORD OF MUHAMMAD ALI

MUHAMMAD ALI
(Cassius Marcellius Clay, Jr.)
(The Louisville Lip)
Born, January 17, 1942, Louisville, Ky. Weight, 186–230 lbs.
Height, 6 ft. 3 in.
1959 National AAU Light Heavyweight Champion
1960 National AAU Light Heavyweight Champion
1960 Olympic Light Heavyweight Gold Medalist

1960

DATE	OPPONENT	LOCATION	DECISION & ROUND	
Oct. 29	Tunny Hunsaker	Louisville	Win	6
Dec. 27	Herb Siler	Miami Beach	Knockout	4

1961

DATE	OPPONENT	LOCATION	DECISION & ROUND	
Jan. 17	Tony Esperti	Miami Beach	Knockout	3
Feb. 7	Jim Robinson	Miami Beach	Knockout	1
Feb. 21	Donnie Fleeman	Miami Beah	Knockout	7
Apr. 19	Lamar Clark	Louisville	Knockout	2
June 26	Duke Sabedong	Las Vegas	Win	10
July 22	Alonzo Johnson	Louisville	Win	10
Oct. 7	Alex Miteff	Louisville	Knockout	6
Nov. 29	Winilli Beananoff	Louisville	Knockout	7

1962

Feb. 10	Sonny Banks	New York	Knockout	4
Feb. 28	Don Warner	Miami Beach	Knockout	4
Apr. 23	George Logan	Los Angeles	Knockout	4
May 19	Billy Daniels	New York	Knockout	7
July 20	Alejandro Lavorante	Los Angeles	Knockout	5
Nov. 15	Archie Moore	Los Angeles	Knockout	4

1963

Jan. 24	Charlie Powell	Pittsburgh	Knockout	3
Mar. 13	Doug Jones	New York	Win	10
June 18	Henry Cooper	London	Knockout	5

1964

| Feb. 25 | Sonny Liston | Miami Beach | Knockout | 7 |

(Won World Heavyweight Title)

1965

| May 25 | Sonny Liston | Lewiston | Knockout | 1 |

(Retained World Heavyweight Title)

July 31	Jimmy Ellis	SanJuan	Exh.	3
July 31	Cody James	San Juan	Exh.	3
Aug. 16	Cody James	Gothenburg	Exh.	2
Aug. 16	Jimmy Ellis	Gothenburg	Exh.	2
Aug. 20	Jimmy Ellis	London	Exh.	2
Aug. 20	Cody Jones	Paisley	Exh.	4
Nov. 22	Floyd Patterson	Las Vegas	Knockout	12

(Retained World Heavyweight Title)

1968

Mar. 29	George Chuvalo	Toronto	Win	15
	(Retained World Heavyweight Title)			
May 21	Henry Cooper	London	Knockout	6
	(Retained World Heavyweight Title)			
Aug. 6	Brian London	London	Knockout	3
	(Retained World Heavyweight Title)			
Sept. 10	Karl Mildenberger	Frankfurt	Knockout	12
	(Retained World Heavywieght Title)			
Nov. 14	Cleveland Williams	Houston	Knockout	3
	(Retained World Heavyweight Title)			

1967

Feb. 6	Ernest Terrell	Houston	Win	15
	(Retained World Heavyweight Title)			
Mar. 22	Zora Folley	New York	Knockout	7
	(Retained World Heavyweight Title)			
June 15	Alvin (Blue) Lewis	Detroit	Exh.	3
June 15	Orvill Qualls	Detroit	Exh.	3

1968–1969

(Inactive)

1970

Feb. 3	Announced retirement			
Oct. 26	Jerry Quarry	Atlanta	Knockout	3
Dec. 7	Oscar Bonavena	New York	Knockout	15

1971

Mar. 8	Joe Frazier	New York	Knockout	3
	(For World Heavyweight Title)			
June 25	J.D. McCauley	Dayton	Exh.	2
June 25	Eddie Brooks	Dayton	Exh.	3
June 25	Rufus Brassel	Dayton	Exh.	3
June 30	Alex Mack	Charleston	Exh.	3
June 30	Eddie Brooks	Charleston	Exh.	4
July 26	Jimmy Ellis	Houston	Knockout	12
	Won Vacant NABF Heavyweight Title)			
Aug. 21	Lancer Johnson	Caracas	Exh.	4
Aug. 21	Eddie Brooks	Caracas	Exh.	4
Aug. 23	Lancer Johnson	Port of Spain	Exh.	4
Aug. 23	Eddie Brooks	Port of Spain	Exh.	4
Nov. 6	James Summerville	Buenos Aires	Exh.	5
Nov. 17	Buster Mathis	Houston	Win	12
	(Retained NABF Heavyweight Title)			
Dec. 26	Jurgen Blin	Zurich	Knockout	7

1972

Apr. 1	Mac Foster	Tokyo	Win	15
May 1	George Chuvalo	Vancouver	Win	12
	(Retained NABF Heavyweight Title)			
June 27	Jerry Quarry	Las Vegas	Knockout	7
	(Retained NABF Heavyweight Title)			
July 1	Lonnie Bennett	Los Angeles	Exh.	2
July 1	Eddie Jones	Los Angeles	Exh.	2
July 1	Billy Ryan	Los Angeles	Exh.	2
July 1	Charley James	Los Angeles	Exh.	2
July 1	Rahanam Ali	Los Angeles	Exh.	2
July 19	Alvin (Blue) Lewis	Dublin	Knockout	11
Aug. 24	Obie English	Baltimore	Exh.	4
Aug. 24	Ray Anderson	Baltimore	Exh.	2
Aug. 24	Alonzo Johnson	Baltimore	Exh.	2
Aug. 24	George Hill	Baltimore	Exh.	2
Aug. 28	Alonzo Johnson	Cleveland	Exh.	2
Aug. 28	Amos Johnson	Cleveland	Exh.	2
Sept. 20	Floyd Patterson	New York	Knockout	7
	(Retained NABF Heavyweight Title)			
Oct. 11	John (Dino) Denis	Boston	Exh.	2
Oct. 11	Cliff McDonald	Boston	Exh.	2
Oct. 11	Doug Kirk	Boston	Exh.	2
Oct. 11	Ray Anderson	Boston	Exh.	2
Oct. 11	Paul Raymond	Boston	Exh.	2
Nov. 21	Bob Foster	Stateline	Knockout	8
	(Retained NABF Heavyweight Title)			

1973

Feb. 14	Joe Bugner	Las Vegas	Win	12
Mar. 31	Ken Norton	San Diego	L	12

(Lost NABF Heavyweight Title)

Sept. 10	Ken Norton	Los Angeles	Win	12

(Regained NABF Heavyweight Title)

Oct. 20	Rudi Lubbera	Djkarta	Win	12

(Retained NABF Heavyweight Title)

Oct. 30	George Foreman	Kinshara	Knockout	8

(Regained World Heavyweight Title)

1975

Mar. 24	Chuck Wepner	Cleveland	Knockout	15

(Retained World Heavyweight Title)

May 16	Ron Lyle	Las Vegas	Knockout	11

(Retained World Heavyweight Title)

July 1	Joe Bugner	Kuala Lumpur	Win	15

(Retained World Heavyweight Title)

Oct. 1	Joe Frazier	Manila	Knockout	14

(Retained World Heavyweight Title)

1976

Feb. 20	Jean Pierre Cooperman	San Juan	Knockout	5

(Retained World Heavyweight Title)

Apr. 30	Jimmy Young	Landover	Win	15

(Retained World Heavyweight Title)

May 24	Richard Dunn	Munich	Knockout	5

(Retained World Heavyweight Title)

June 25	Antonio Inoki	Tokyo	Exh. D	15

(Above match was the boxer against a wrestler.)

Sept. 28	Ken Norton	New York	Win	15

(Retained World Heavyweight Title)

1977

Jan. 29	Peter Fuller	Boston	Exh.	4
Jan. 29	Winalter Haines	Boston	Exh.	1
Jan. 29	Jeyy Houston	Boston	Exh.	2
Jan. 29	Ron Drinkwater	Boston	Exh.	2
Jan. 29	Matt Ross	Boston	Exh.	2
Jan. 29	Frank Smith	Boston	Exh.	1
May 16	Alfredo Evangelista	Landover	Win	15
	(Retained World Heavyweight Title)			
Sept. 29	Earnie Shavers	New York	Win	15
	(Retained World Heavyweight Title)			
Dec. 2	Scott LeDoux	Chicago	Exh.	5

1978

Feb. 15	Leon Spinks	Las Vegas	L	15
	(Lost World Heavyweight Title)			
Sept. 15	Leon Spinks	New Orleans	Win	15
	(Regained World Heavyweight Title)			

1979

Announced retirement

1980

Oct. 2	Larry Holmes	Las Vegas	Knockout	11
	(For World Heavyweight Title)			

1981

Dec. 11	Trevor Berdick	Nassau	L	10

INDEX

194

195

PICTURE CREDITS

ABC: pp. 8, 50, 104; NBC: pp. 11, 74, 151, 152; UPI/Bettmann: pp. 14, 20, 33, 35, 68, 138; Eddie Brandt's Saturday Matinee: pp. 17, 24, 25, (Robert Grant) 95, 156, 173; James Jeffrey; pp. 174, 180, 187; Columbia Pictures: 28, 124; Willie Dooley: pp. 36, 71, 128; Players International Libray: pp. 41, 44, 62, 53, 77, 82, 109, 112, 113, 144; United Artists; pp. 87, 90; HBO; p. 96; Charles Adams; p. 132; Guy Crowder; p. 164

CHRISTOPHER RICCELLA was born in Hollywood, California, reared in Las Vegas, Nevada and has an advanced degree in literature from the University of Southern California. He specializes in writing non-fiction for young adults but vows to "write a novel someday." He currently lives in Studio City, California.

PSEUDO COOL
BY JOSEPH E. GREEN

A Novel of today's black, wealthy and privileged youth

Five black seniors at a prestigious west coast university each have a secret. one sells herself to pay the expensive tuition; one drinks heavily and sleeps with white girls in an attempt to disinheit his blackness; another is gay, and living in the closet; another is a poor girl adopted into a high society family; two believe they were responsible for a friend's death. Each is thinking only of graduation. Each believes that the answer to the problems that plague them lies just the other side of college life

Pseudo Cool is a tough, shocking first novel in the genre of the sensational bestseller, Less Than Zero. Joseph E. Green is a student at Stanford University.

HOLLOWAY HOUSE PUBLISHING CO.
8060 MELROSE AVE., LOS ANGELES, CA 90046

Gentlemen: I enclose $_____ ☐ cash, ☐ check, ☐ money order, payment in full for books ordered. I understand that if I am not completely satisfied, I may return my order within 10 days for a complete refund. (Add .90 cents per order to cover postage. California residents add 6½% sales tax. Please allow four weeks for delivery. ☐ **BH 329-7 $2.95 Pseduo Cool**

Name _____

Address _____

City_____State_____Zip_____

TRIUMPH & TRAGEDY
The True Story of the
THE SUPREMES

By Marianne Ruuth

No Holds Barred!

Marianne Ruuth interviewed former members of The Supremes, friends and associates for an in-depth look at those three young women that all of American fell in love with back in the 1960s. They were: Florence Ballard ("the shy one"), Mary Wilson ("the one many considered to be the most talented") and Diana Ross ("the one determined to become a star"), all from Detroit and all terribly innocent in the beginning. Florence became the figure of tragedy: She died very young, living on welfare. Mary, still performing, found something of a normal life for a star. . .and we all know that Diana realized her ambition of becoming a Superstar. Now read the real story behind the headlines and the gossip!

HOLLOWAY HOUSE PUBLISHING CO.
8060 MELROSE AVE., LOS ANGELES, CA 90046

Gentlemen: I enclose $_____ ☐ cash, ☐ check, ☐ money order, payment in full for books ordered. I understand that if I am not completely satisfied, I may return my order within 10 days for a complete refund. (Add 75 cents per order to cover postage. California residents add 6½% sales tax. Please allow three weeks for delivery.)

■ BH725-X TRIUMPH & TRAGEDY $2.95

Name _____

Address _____

City _____ State _____ Zip _____

THE DOWRY

By Ginger Whitaker
Few Things Come Without A Price. Love Is One Of Them.

Carrie Brown was young and beautiful, and a mystery the townspeople couldn't figure out. Left motherless at birth, she was sheltered her whole life by an over-protective and bitter father, the deacon of the Deliverance Church. The townspeople observed her from a distance, never really knowing her, only knowing about her. One person, Jimmy McCormack, paid particular attention to Carrie. For Jimmy, she was the answer to the age old gnawing in his heart. He would do anything to have Carrie Brown. Anything. Even buy her. But what Jimmy ends up paying and what Carrie ends up getting, are not what either had expected.

☐ BH 332-7 **THE DOWRY** $3.50

HOLLOWAY HOUSE PUBLISHING CO.
8060 MELROSE AVE., LOS ANGELES, CA 90046

Gentlemen: I enclose $_____ ☐ cash, ☐ check, ☐ money order, payment in full for books ordered. I understand that if I am not completely satisfied, I may return my order within 10 days for a complete refund. (Add 75 cents per order to cover postage. California residents add 6½% sales tax. Please allow three weeks for delivery.)

Name _____

Address _____

City _____ **State** _____ **Zip** _____

TO KILL A BLACK MAN

By Louis E. Lomax

A compelling dual biography of the two men who changed America's way of thinking—Malcolm X and Martin Luther King, Jr.

Louis E. Lomax was a close friend to both Malcolm X and Dr. Martin Luther King, Jr. In this dual biography, he includes much that Malcolm X did not tell in his autobiography and dissects Malcolm's famous letters. Lomax writes with the sympathy and understanding of a friend but he is also quick to point out the shortcomings of both Dr. King and Malcolm X—and what he believed was the reasons for their failure to achieve their goals and to obtain the full support of all their people. And he does not hesitate in pointing a finger at those he believes to be responsible for the deaths of his friends. "A valuable addition to the available information on the murders of Martin Luther King, Jr. and Malcolm X," says the *Litterair Passport*. Louis Lomax gained national prominence with such books as *The Black Revolt, When The Word Is Given*, and *To Kill A Black Man*. At the time of his death in an automobile accident he was a professor at Hofstra University.

HOLLOWAY HOUSE PUBLISHING CO.

8060 MELROSE AVE., LOS ANGELES, CALIF. 90046

Gentlemen: I enclose _____ ☐ cash, ☐ check, ☐ money order, payment in full for books ordered. I understand that if I am not completely satisfied, I may return my order within 10 days for a complete refund. (Add 75c per order to cover postage. California residents add 6½% tax. Please allow three weeks for delivery.)

☐ BH731-4 **TO KILL A BLACK MAN** $3.25

Name _____

Address _____

City _____ State _____ Zip _____

REUNION

By Mark Allen Boone

The Fascinating Story of One Man's Fight to Regain His Family's Honor. . .

Reunion is the story of two friends, and one man's determination to find his origin. Mostly, it's a story about friendship—the kind that goes way beyond family and blood; the kind that lives forever. Levi Merriweather and Wesley Luckett are such friends. They're the best of friends. They shared everything, even the same woman. But friends sometimes grow apart. And then something happens that brings them back together.

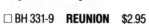

☐ BH 331-9 **REUNION** $2.95

HOLLOWAY HOUSE PUBLISHING CO.
8060 MELROSE AVE., LOS ANGELES, CA 90048

Gentlemen: I enclose $_____ ☐ cash, ☐ check, ☐ money order, payment in full for books ordered. I understand that if I am not completely satisfied, I may return my order within 10 days for a complete refund. (Add 75 cents per order to cover postage. California residents add 6½% sales tax. Please allow three weeks for delivery.)

Name _____

Address _____

City _____ **State** _____ **Zip** _____

The Saga of Five
Generations of

A MISSISSIPPI FAMILY

By Barbara Johnson
With Mary Sikora

A stirring tale of one family's rise from slavery to respect: From poverty to relative comfort, *A Mississippi Family* is, like *Roots* based on those things remembered—deaths, weddings, tragedy, tears and laughter—and passed on to generation after generation. Barbara Johnson, born and raised in central Mississippi where most of the story takes place, has done a remarkable job of turning oral history into a wonderful book. The Elams and many of their descendants are unforgettable characters, ones that you won't soon forget . . .and will stir warm memories of your own.

HOLLOWAY HOUSE PUBLISHING CO.
8060 MELROSE AVE., LOS ANGELES, CA 90046

Gentlemen: I enclose $_____ ☐ cash, ☐ check, ☐ money order, payment in full for books ordered. I understand that if I am not completely satisfied, I may return my order within 10 days for a complete refund. (Add 75 cents per order to cover postage. California residents add 6½% sales tax. Please allow three weeks for delivery.)

☐ BH272-X A MISSISSIPPI FAMILY $2.50

Name _____

Address _____

City _____ State _____ Zip _____

JESSE JACKSON

By Eddie Stone

An Intimate Portrait of the Most Charismatic Man in American Politics

He's dynamic, charming, intelligent and has more charisma than any man to rocket into the American political arena since John F. Kennedy. One of the country's most popular black leaders, he is not without his critics. To many he is just too flamboyant, others find his political ideas somewhat vague, still others call him a blatant opportunist. Nevertheless he has proven he can pull in the votes whether it's in Vermont, or Mississippi, or Michigan. Jackson will play a major—and far reaching—role in American politics in the years to come.

HOLLOWAY HOUSE PUBLISHING CO.
8060 MELROSE AVE., LOS ANGELES, CA 90046

Gentlemen: I enclose $_____ ☐ cash, ☐ check, ☐ money order, payment in full for books ordered. I understand that if I am not completely satisfied, I may return my order within 10 days for a complete refund. (Add 90 cents per book to cover postage. California residents add 6½% sales tax. Please allow three weeks for delivery.) **840-X JESSE JACKSON $3.95**

Name _____

Address _____

City _____ State _____ Zip _____